"This third edition of Morrie Warshawski's classic on raising money for filmmaking, *Shaking the Money Tree*, is a treasure chest of time-tested fundraising wisdom, insight, and down-to-earth guidance you can put to work today. It's chock full of examples and advice, much of it in the words of highly successful filmmakers themselves. Buy this book without delay!"
> — Mal Warwick , author of *Fundraising When Money Is Tight*

"This book is a monumental contribution of knowledge for filmmakers everywhere. It's a masterpiece that guides you confidently from the concept to the completion of your film."
> — Carole Dean, From the Heart Productions, author of *The Art of Film Funding*

"Morrie Warshawski's advice is valuable to all people, in all fields, not just independent film. He is as much a life coach as a consultant to indie filmmakers. I thoroughly enjoyed this new book and look forward to using it regularly, not only for the filmmakers I coach, but for myself."
> — Cynthia Close, Executive Director, Documentary Educational Resources

"Morrie Warshawski has done it again! Just when you think he couldn't improve on his terrific book, *Shaking the Money Tree,* he has done just that. With this new 3rd edition Warshawski tells us everything we need to know about raising money in these difficult times. If you follow Morrie's guidelines you have a better chance of raising money for your project and propelling your career forward. I don't know a single filmmaker who couldn't benefit from reading this book."
> — Kelley Baker, The Angry Filmmaker (*www.angryfilmmaker .com*)

"Timely, cogent, clear and practical, this new edition of *Shaking the Money Tree* builds on timeless advice to include the new realities of fundraising in a networked world. With case studies and advice direct from pros throughout the field, it is just the resource for sparking and maintaining any filmmaker's fundraising momentum."
> — Sally Jo Fifer, President, CEO, Independent Television Service (ITVS)

D1115553

"This is the perfect fundraising book for filmmakers. Covering everything from pitching in person to fundraising on the web, this new edition is a must-own for every filmmaker — and actually for anyone raising funds, be it for a film or for their organization. While the book is geared towards filmmakers, the advice is relevant to anyone raising money in the arts. The sample grants in the appendix are worth the cost alone. This is the third time I've read this book, and I learn something new with every edition."

— Brian Newman, CEO, Tribeca Film Institute

"Although specifically written for film and video artists, *Shaking the Money Tree* offers succinct and excellent advice that is applicable to artists in *all* fields. Morrie Warshawski has a relaxed and human-friendly writing style. His insights are on target and should resonate with those working in all arts disciplines."

— Caroll Michels, Career Coach and Artist-Advocate, author of *How to Survive and Prosper as an Artist: Selling Yourself Without Selling Your Soul*

"During these difficult economic times, Morrie Warshawski's *Shaking the Money Tree* is indispensable reading. This is a money marketing book that not only tells you where the money is but provides you with practical, popular, and even not-so-popular ways to access it. Obviously written by someone who knows the ropes when it comes to 'creative financing' for movies, *Money Tree* promises to bear fruit if you put into action the several strategies Warshawski provides in this comprehensive guide."

— Jeffrey M. Freedman, Resident Alien Productions, VP Development/Producer, screenwriter (*Vivaldi*)

"Morrie Warshawski's knowledge of fundraising is as essential now as it was when his first edition was published — maybe even more so. The world has changed dramatically — the economy, technology, even philanthropy — and Morrie has kept pace with those changes. A strategy for fundraising is a must and Morrie lays it out for you brilliantly. New filmmakers *and* seasoned pros: pay close attention!"

— Alyce Myatt, Executive Director, Grantmakers in Film + Electronic Media

SHAKING THE MONEY TREE

The Art of

GETTING GRANTS and DONATIONS

for FILM and VIDEO PROJECTS

3rd Edition

MORRIE WARSHAWSKI

MICHAEL WIESE PRODUCTIONS

Published by Michael Wiese Productions
12400 Ventura Blvd. #1111
Studio City, CA 91604
(818) 379-8799, (818) 986-3408 (FAX)
mw@mwp.com
www.mwp.com

Cover design by MWP
Interior design by William Morosi
Copyedited by Paul Norlen
Printed by McNaughton & Gunn

Library of Congress Cataloging-in-Publication Data
Warshawski, Morrie.
Shaking the money tree : the art of getting grants and donations for
film and video projects / Morrie Warshawski. -- 3rd ed.
    p. cm.
Includes bibliographical references.
ISBN 978-1-932907-66-7
1. Motion picture industry--United States--Finance. 2. Video
recordings industry--United States--Finance. I. Title.
PN1993.5.U6W33 2010
791.430973--dc22

                                  2009029580

dedicated (again) to
my three muses
Evy, Leah, and Maura

TABLE OF CONTENTS

x   *Foreword*

xii   *Introduction*

1   *Chapter One*

LAYING THE FOUNDATION: YOUR CAREER

2   First Steps
4   Next Steps
5   Last Steps

9   *Chapter Two*

WHERE'S THE MONEY?

10   Individuals
13   Government
14   Private Foundations
16   Corporations
18   Small Businesses
19   Other Nonprofits
20   Mixing It Up
21   For-Profit

24   *Chapter Three*

PATCHWORK QUILT — PUTTING YOUR PROJECT TOGETHER

24   The Story That Had to Be Told
26   Audience/Community
29   Distribution
33   Good Company
34   Good Timing
36   Money Matters
39   Nonprofit — a Definition
40   Your Umbrella — The Fiscal Sponsor

43 *Chapter Four*

GETTING PERSONAL — INDIVIDUAL DONORS

44 The Pitch
48 Qualify the Donor
51 One-on-One
53 Fundraising Houseparties
56 Letters
57 The World Wide Web and Its Tentacles

64 *Chapter Five*

THE PAPER TRAIL — FOUNDATIONS AND GOVERNMENT AGENCIES

65 Research
67 Your Approach: It's Personal
74 Writing the Proposal
77 Elements of a Full Grant Proposal
92 Last Calls

97 *Chapter Six*

ALL THE REST

97 Alternative Strategies
103 Students
106 Going Corporate
109 The Corner Store
110 Good Housekeeping
113 Morrie's Maxims

115 # APPENDIX

115 Sample Grant #1 — ITVS
128 Sample Grant #2 — *Behind the Velvet Curtain*
168 Select Bibliography — Publications and Helpful Web Sites

171 *About the Author*

FOREWORD

One of the most important ideas in Morrie Warshawski's *Shaking the Money Tree* is that there is no one way to finance a film; every filmmaker has to go to far and unfamiliar lengths to fund a movie. I learned this the hard way. My first film, *Harlan County USA*, was a special but difficult one to make. We followed a coal miners union in the midst of a bitter labor strike. These men and women were fighting for very basic rights, and they were putting their lives on the line to secure the compensation, benefits, and protection they deserved.

Whenever I had a break in filming, I was running back to New York City to raise money for the movie. Independent filmmaking wasn't yet as developed as it has become. More importantly, there wasn't a book like Morrie's to guide you along in the process. I was at a loss for what to do. I knew there were grants available for filmmakers like me, but I didn't know how to approach them. I finally decided that the only way to ever know what these organizations were looking for was to ask. And so I called those foundations and just asked them questions, talked with them, tried to understand what they looked for in an application. I would consider our discussions and apply until the grants started coming through. It took a long time and was very frustrating. It was a hard but valuable lesson to go through this desperate limbo period. I realized that you have to be bold and creative when looking for funds, and I'm glad I finally learned it when I did.

The very lessons I had to learn on *Harlan County USA* are discussed brilliantly in *Shaking the Money Tree*'s 170 pages, and I wish it had been there for me when I was making my first film. Morrie's illuminating insights into dealing with foundations balance the ambition necessary to dreaming up your film with the practicality required to connect with and impress foundation judges with your vision. He goes on to explore the details of how to focus your goals for your film and how to target the right foundations to get your movie made and seen. *Shaking the Money Tree* is full of lists of organizations you can make contact with, samples of applications that were approved for funding, and priceless testimony from film-makers who have been successful in raising money for themselves. There's no question that this will be helpful for anyone who reads it. This 3rd Edition is a great resource for exploiting some new technological avenues for funding your film. Morrie details how the Internet can not only be a resource for finding information about foundations, but can also serve as a tool for soliciting funds and as an the avenue through which to show your film.

Shaking the Money Tree is a special book that I think filmmakers of all levels can benefit from. It's thoroughly researched and lucidly written, emphasizing that with focus, perseverance, and resourcefulness, you can bring to fruition the stories you are trying to tell. Clearly, this is a slow and difficult economic time, and these lulls always fall hardest on the independents, but the basic tenets of *Shaking the Money Tree* ring true for all times – you have to be imaginative, you have to be patient, and you have to try everything in order to get your film made. This is the tradition of independent cinema and will continue to be here for as long as there are independent artists at work.

Reading this book will remind independents that with vision and commitment to making a film, it can be done. Morrie has worked for decades as a consultant and facilitator — he understands the tremendous emotional investment that filmmakers put into their films. His book is evidence of the tremendous care, attention, and wisdom Morrie poured into his book. As a filmmaker, you can trust that Morrie has your best interests at heart. And I greatly appreciate his efforts in putting together this invaluable book for the generations of filmmakers to come.

Barbara Kopple, two-time Academy Award–winning director and producer (*Harlan County USA, American Dream*)

But when I said that nothing had been done I erred in one important matter. We had definitely committed ourselves and were halfway out of our ruts. We had put down our passage money — booked a sailing to Bombay. This may sound too simple, but is great in consequence. Until one is committed, there is hesitance, the chance to draw back, always ineffectiveness. Concerning all acts of initiative (and creation) there is one elementary truth, the ignorance of which kills countless ideas and splendid plans: that the moment one definitely commits oneself, then Providence moves, too.

All sorts of things occur to help one that would never have otherwise occurred. A whole stream of events issues from the decision, raising in one's favour all manner of unforeseen incidents, meetings, and material assistance, which no man would have dreamed could have come his way. I learned a deep respect for one of Goethe's couplets:

"Whatever you can do or dream you can, begin it.
Boldness has genius, power and magic in it."

W. H. Murray in *The Scottish Himalaya Expedition*

INTRODUCTION

An old man was dying. He was surrounded by his children, and as he lay on his death bed, his last words were, "I've buried a treasure on the farm—" and he died. The children picked up shovels and started digging up the ground, but try as they might, they could not find the buried treasure. The next year, however, they had the best harvest the farm had ever seen.

Fundraising for independent film projects is an exhilarating, time-intensive, difficult and frustrating endeavor. The filmmaker is exploring the terrain for treasure wherever she can, often coming up empty-handed. What I have come to understand is that, even though short-term results can be slim, over the long term the process of fundraising makes for a better film, and a filmmaker who is more connected to her community.

The first edition of this book appeared in 1994. On a lark, I had called Michael Wiese to pitch an idea I had for a book that would teach independent filmmakers the ins and outs of fundraising. I expected him to ask me for a full proposal with a table of contents, sample chapters, and marketing data. Instead, he greenlighted the project on the spot, and we've been off and rolling ever since. In 2003 I completely rewrote the book for a 2nd edition. Now, fifteen years after the first edition appeared, I've created a brand new 3rd edition.

As I write this introduction, the nation and the world are in the midst of the worst financial crisis in memory. The normal difficulties inherent in fundraising have been magnified. This only intensifies the importance of the advice you will find in this new edition. I have always warned filmmakers that they face stiff competition for support. Now, more than ever, the savvy filmmaker must be very aware of all the options — both traditional and alternative — available for fundraising, and must enter each arena in a prepared and professional manner. In an added bit of irony, my eldest daughter — against my advice! — recently entered the field and is busy fundraising for a documentary on young filmmakers in Rwanda (*www.inflatablefilm.com*).

It is both a new world and an old world. Some things have not and will not change — the need for researching every funder to be approached, the demands of foundations and government funders for exemplary grant proposals, the call from corporations for a well-defined audience, the desire of individual donors to be involved with projects that will make a real difference. Other things have changed dramatically — the Internet has become much more important in the fundraising process (Web sites, blogs, social networking sites), filmmakers are being forced to be more entrepreneurial than ever and explore multiple sources for support, funders are demanding more proof that projects will actually reach an audience and engage a community.

This new edition takes these new realities into account. One major change I have made is to follow my own advice about becoming "interdependent." Throughout the book there are new sidebars by respected people in the field who have advice to give in their areas of expertise. These are people who work in the trenches, and I know you are going to benefit from their words of wisdom. They've been busy digging up the ground for you!

For the novice, student, and emerging filmmaker, this book will help form the foundation of your work as a media artist who must also work as a fundraiser. The book will help ensure that you don't make the mistakes common to being "green" in the field. For the mid-career filmmaker, the book will reinforce information you already have, encourage your resolve to do things you've promised to do but haven't, and will give you a grab bag of new ideas for fundraising from other professionals in the field. For the experienced and seasoned filmmaker, this book will help jumpstart any stalled career and fundraising plans, and perhaps provide some inspiration.

Chapter One is about your career. You may be tempted to skip this part of the book and jump ahead into the sections on fundraising, but don't! The advice in this chapter forms the foundation for all the work you will ever do in fundraising.

Chapter Two provides a quick overview of all the sources of funds for independent noncommercial projects, and gives you an "upside/downside" view of each.

Chapter Three concentrates all the things in your project that must be solidified before fundraising begins. These are the basic questions and issues that all funders will want resolved before you ask them for money.

Chapter Four takes a close look at all the ways you can raise money from individuals and will help you hone just the right techniques for the perfect "ask" whether it is in person, at a houseparty, or through the mail.

Chapter Five covers everything you need to know about creating the perfect grant proposal so that you can approach foundations and government agencies.

Chapter Six covers the rest of the territory, including an extensive section on alternative fundraising methods and the Internet, as well as corporations, small businesses, and a note on fundraising for student projects.

There is only one reason I keep putting energy into this book — *you*, the independent filmmaker, are creating stories that must be told, that must be heard, and that are making a significant difference to the quality of our lives. Your commitment to these stories is so deep that you are willing to make tremendous sacrifices (financial, personal, professional) in order to bring them to life. This book is devoted to helping ease that process as much as possible.

Let me end this introduction with special heartfelt THANKS to all of the following friends and colleagues who helped me make this new edition possible: Howard Aaron, Claire Aguilar, Ralph Arlyck, Robert Bahar, Diana Barrett, Peter Broderick, Marissa Carlisle, Almudena Carracedo, Nikki Chase, Dan Cogan, Arwen Currey, Jenny Deller, Paul Devlin, Alice Elliott, Judith Erlich, Sonia Feigenbaum, Peter Frumkin, Michael Gibson, Julie Goldman, Rick Goldsmith, Jonathan Joiner, Barbara Kopple, Ken Lee, Ruby Lerner, Wendy Levy, Robert Martin, Michele Meek, Tamara Perkins, Ashley Phelps, Julia Reichert, Andy Robinson, Fernanda Rossi, Slava Rubin, Shaady Salehi, Ellen Schneider, Mike Shiley, Tiffany Shlain, Michele Turner-Salleo and the San Francisco Film Society, Tricia van Klaveren, Mal Warwick, Evy Warshawski, Hunter Weeks, David Weinstein, Michael Wiese.

Please feel free to contact me with your reactions to this book and with your success stories. Best of luck in having all your hard work bear fruit.

Morrie Warshawski
Napa, California
January 2010
www.warshawski.com

CHAPTER ONE

LAYING THE FOUNDATION:
Your Career

Once, when someone asked jazz pianist/composer Thelonious Monk how he managed to get a certain special sound out of the piano, Monk pointed to the keyboard and said: "It can't be any new note. When you look at the keyboard, all the notes are there already. But if you mean a note enough, it will sound different. You got to pick the notes you really mean!"

Filmmaking is a funny business. Part art, part business. Neither fish nor fowl. How does a professional fashion a career in this hybrid environment where the formal training is primarily concerned with technique and aesthetics, but rarely with business and career development skills?

When a filmmaker comes to me for advice it's almost always because of a problem with funding — or rather a problem with a lack of funding. I work almost exclusively with artists in the noncommercial sector who are doing the type of projects that need grants and donations for support. What I have discovered over the years is that funding problems are almost always rooted in a basic set of unresolved career issues. This work has led me to a system of consulting that focuses on helping professionals with career development basics that, in turn, affect every aspect of their work, including fundraising.

1

Below is a quick summary of the main points of my approach to career development work.

FIRST STEPS

The "first step" my clients must accomplish is to identify their set of **Core Values** — those immutable values that are inherent in their daily lives and infuse all the interactions they have with others, both personal and professional. We are stuck with our values, our basic set of beliefs. They follow us wherever we go and dictate how we respond to our significant others, how we act in teams, how we drive our cars or cook our meals. Since we are stuck with these values, the important thing for a filmmaker to do is to recognize these values, bring them to the surface, and broadcast them proudly. In this manner, values serve as a strong attractor — and a strong detractor — as a filmmaker moves through the professional world, picking the projects and people with whom she wants to work. Because core values are inescapable, they have become a more and more important part of my work with all clients. My own core values are: creativity, tolerance, thoughtfulness, and transparency. Filmmakers I have worked with recently have listed the following values: mentoring, curiosity, honesty, human spirit, humor, intelligence, courage.

The next thing I ask every new client to do is to create a **Mission Statement** — a short, succinct enumeration of their *raison d'etre*. Why are you a filmmaker? What are you trying to accomplish with your work? The filmmaker has to be able to articulate this for herself, and for everyone she meets. This encapsulates the heart of her work. The Mission Statement also helps the filmmaker make day-to-day decisions about what projects to accept or reject, and how to apportion time to be most effective.

The most important aspect of the mission statement is its ability to help the filmmaker articulate and commit to a unique sense of purpose that keeps her centered, and broadcasts to all potential funders and clients that this is a person who is serious about her work and knows what she wants to accomplish. No one wants to work with or fund a filmmaker who is unclear about this central issue.

I had a client once who was very gifted and had created a few excellent award-winning documentaries, but was having no luck fundraising for her next project. As we began our work I asked for her Mission Statement. She said that she didn't have one. We then explored how she was approaching funders. As it happens, she was going to funders and saying, "I'm an accomplished filmmaker. I just want funds to do documentary work, and I'm willing to make a film about anything that is of interest to your foundation." It took a while for me to convince her that her approach was all wrong. She needed to be very clear about why she was making films, and what she hoped to accomplish, otherwise funders would not take her seriously. She took the time to create a Mission Statement that conveyed her true interests, then matched that with a project that she very much wanted to accomplish. After a year of fundraising she was able to raise over $1 million for her next film.

Here is a note I received from filmmaker Alice Elliott (director of the Academy Award–nominated documentary *The Collector of Bedford Street*):

> *Dear Morrie,*
> *Just a brief testimonial. Since I've started saying my per-sonal mission statement whenever I speak, and adding it to my e-mails, funding opportunities have sort of jumped up in my lap. It's very neat.*
> *Yours,*
> *Alice*

Alice had gone through a number of iterations of her mission statement. An early version was: "Creating art that shows us how to live together with humor, tolerance, and compassion." After some consideration it became: "Leading social change by revealing the big stories hidden in the human heart." If you visit her Web site, *www.welcomechange.org*, you'll find her mission statement right at the top of the home page.

After creating a mission statement, I ask every client to create a **Vision Statement.** My instructions are to pick a point in the future (at least three years out) and envision as specifically as possible what your life as a filmmaker will be like in that future. I often have my clients draw a picture of this future, and then go back into the picture to identify items/accomplishments that are more important than others.

The Vision Statement is a powerful tool for energizing the movement of a career, and for giving focus to the accomplishments that mean more to a filmmaker than other things. The filmmaker's vision may well change over the years, but it always provides the filmmaker with a set of strong images around which she can create a plan of action. It's the vision that allows you to become strategic.

Two years after giving my "Jumpstarting Your Career" workshop at Seattle's 911 Media Arts Center, I received a call from one of the attendees. I remembered him well because during the workshop he had drawn a particularly vivid and simple set of vision drawings — one showed his present reality as a person sitting by himself in a theater watching a group of people working on a stage, and the second drawing of his future vision showed a theater full of people watching him working on the stage with a crew and actors. "I just called," he said "because I found that drawing I did a couple of years ago and realized that I've gone from being an independent and isolated filmmaker to someone who is working at an agency with lots of creative people, and I'd completely forgotten that this was my dream." Once the vision is located it can have a powerful pull on a filmmaker's next steps.

NEXT STEPS

Once the filmmaker settles all the issues of Mission, Vision, and Values, she can move on to designing a healthy path toward career development. At this point, it helps tremendously if the filmmaker can identify just a few **Major Goals** — both short-term (six to twelve months into the future) and long-term. These goals, on the short-term side, must be reasonable and achievable goals. And whenever possible, they should be goals that can be quantified (e.g., "Finish one short film per year for the next three years" or "Learn how to do digital editing using XYZ software on my home computer within the next five months").

The goals should be in alignment with the vision the filmmaker created for the future. All the goals should be directed at helping the filmmaker make a difference to her career, even if that difference is a small one. You want to create some momentum forward, so even small steps are important.

One exercise I often give is to have the filmmaker create two lists of actions: "Five Quick Wins" and "Five Bold Moves." The quick wins help to define actions that can take place in the short term and give the filmmaker some quick successes, which are very important for morale. The bold moves help the filmmaker identify larger and riskier actions that, if taken, can make a major difference to a career. The bold moves are harder to make, and therefore demand a different level of commitment — one that brings the filmmaker to the very center of how serious she may or may not be about her professed choice of career and vision for the future.

If goals are in place, and the filmmaker is very grounded in a career direction that she feels very strongly about, then it's time to consider one of the basic facts of life in filmmaking, and every other profession — the fact that it is other people who help make or break a career. At this point in planning I have clients identify their **Circles of Influence**. Begin by considering the various large areas of career path that you will have to affect or interact with in order to succeed. These might include Studios, Producers, Foundations, Public Television Stations, Cable Networks, and the Press. Next, identify specific organizations and their locations. Then, for each organization identify the names of the people you need to influence. Where you do not know the name, list the title and then find out who fills that position. Now you have a good rich map full of names that you must fold into your *modus operandi* as you begin to pursue your goals. Place these people in your database, make them aware of you, and meet them in person whenever possible.

LAST STEPS

Actually there are no last steps in career development. It's an ongoing process that you will probably take with you into retirement when you replace professional development goals with those of personal growth. What a filmmaker can do to help ensure success is concentrate on a few basic concepts. One is a constant feedback loop of evaluation. The task here is to take regular stock of how you are doing against the goals you have set for yourself. Have you met your targets on time? If not, then what has held you back and how can you adjust either the goal or your performance level to keep moving forward?

Another important aspect of career development is the acquisition of a number of "tools" for your toolkit. News releases, resumes, press clippings of feature articles and reviews, festival awards, video clips, "kudos" letters from prominent people, an attractive Web site and/or blog, participation in social networking sites, a compelling project "pitch" — these are all strategic tools that when used wisely will be a boon to a growing career. Creative professionals have a large arsenal of these tools and use them when appropriate to help pave the path forward.

One of the more difficult art forms to promote is video art. I have had a client for a number of years who is a video artist. When we first met he had already created a small but interesting body of work that was only known by a handful of people. We put together a promotional strategy that fit his temperament and included, among other things: identifying all the people and agencies who were important to his career development; a press release list with street and e-mail addresses; a commitment to sending out news releases every three months; a commitment to creating an attractive postcard for every new work; the creation of a Web site. In the ten years we have worked together his career has taken a quantum leap forward. Of course, it helps that his work is of excellent quality to begin with, but the use of the proper public relations tools have made a tremendous difference.

One last item I must mention, but that is often ignored, is that of an emotional support system. It is very easy for filmmakers to be isolated. That's one reason I've come to dislike the word "independent" and to encourage all my clients to learn to become "interdependent." I cannot overstate the importance of networking, of finding other like-minded people with whom you can share information, trade services, and swap horror stories. Get connected. Create support systems and build in time to network regularly.

IN SUMMARY:

- Identify and broadcast your values
- Clarify and commit to your mission
- Create a clear and compelling vision
- Set ambitious but achievable short- and long-term goals
- Evaluate your progress and adjust your strategies accordingly
- Interact with the key people in the center of your circles of influence
- Develop a strong set of tools for career development
- Network, network, network!

Ruby Lerner — President of Creative Capital, and former Executive Director of the Association of Independent Film and Videomakers (AIVF) — has worked with independent filmmakers for decades. Creative Capital is very invested in helping artists move forward in their professions. Here are some tips from her on career development for filmmakers:

RUBY'S RULES

1. For each project, **always ask yourself: "Who is this for?"** We all want to believe that our work is for the "general public." But for the most part, the general public stays away in droves. By achieving clarity about your "target" audience, you can deploy finite resources in the most effective ways.

2. Understand that **you are not done when you're done.** You may be ready to hand your film over to festivals, distributors, and exhibitors when you finally complete your project, but your work is just beginning. When you start each new film, it is important to ask yourself if you are willing to stay with the project for 12–24 months after its initial public launch. If you don't care enough about the project to make this time commitment, why undertake it in the first place? This is necessary if you expect your work to have impact in the world — and on your future career prospects.

3. **Always be learning from others in your field.** There is a lot of invaluable information to be gleaned from the experiences of your peers. This is true about the continuing development of your craft as well as your career.

(continues)

RUBY'S RULES (cont.)

4. Don't stop there. **Expand your horizons by learning from successes in other sectors.** Read magazines and books, explore Web sites, attend conferences, and take workshops.

5. **Build your own mailing list — aggressively.** Everyone you meet is a potential advocate for your work and a potential supporter. Your mailing list is one of your greatest assets as you move forward through a (hopefully) long and rewarding career. It is also an asset that can be traded with colleagues when it comes time for project promotion.

6. **Make the Internet an integral part of your practice.** This means more than just having an up-to-date Web site; it means having a presence on appropriate social networking sites, and especially, connecting with organizations and entities whose constituencies may have an interest in your project. This extraordinary tool makes it so much easier to stay in touch with your own current supporters about the progress of your projects, but it also creates opportunities to exponentially increase your personal constituency. Some artists are using social networking tools to determine the financial viability of touring to specific locations, by mobilizing personal constituencies on behalf of their projects. Some are using it to do project fundraising. It has become an indispensable way to let your friends and fans know what you are up to.

7. And finally, **never "phone it in."** Ever. Be prepared to maximize every opportunity. For instance, if you are asked to be on a panel, prepare for it, don't see it as something informal to which you can just show up and "wing it." You don't know who could be sitting in the audience who might get excited about your project or vision — if clearly articulated — and who might have concrete ways to help.

Ruby Lerner, President
Creative Capital

CHAPTER TWO

WHERE'S THE MONEY?

"Where is the money?" That's an easy question to answer. There is a simple map to follow for finding money, and it is made up almost exclusively of the following (placed in order of their ranking for giving to all noncommercial endeavors of every type — not just film and video — nationwide):

- ◆ Individuals
- ◆ Government (Federal, State, and Local)
- ◆ Private Foundations
- ◆ Corporations
- ◆ Small Businesses
- ◆ Other Nonprofit Organizations

The filmmaker must remember that he is swimming in a sea of money — surrounded by many sources of funding. The difficult decision is choosing which of these sources is the most appropriate for the filmmaker's personality and for each project so that energy is placed in the right direction. The filmmaker needs to:

- create a fundraising plan
- identify the most appropriate sources for each project
- research each prospect thoroughly, and then
- make the "ask" in the most effective way possible.

There are no deep, dark secrets to fundraising and no set of arcane or insanely difficult skills to acquire. Mainly, fundraising is just plain hard work. One thing that complicates fundraising is that it takes a slightly different set of tools to work in each avenue of possible support. Approaching individuals is different from approaching private foundations. The fundraising letter you send to a corporation will be very different from the one you send to a small business.

This chapter introduces you to the broad categories of possible support and provides an overview of the terrain. I will highlight the "upside" and "downside" of each avenue, list the main ways to research each area, and quickly highlight the means of approach. Later in this book I will be giving much more detail on how to actually conduct your fundraising approaches (e.g., how to write a grant, how to ask an individual for support).

INDIVIDUALS

Upside: Individuals have traditionally represented over 80% of all the donations given to all noncommercial enterprises of all types in the U.S. Individual donors provide the filmmaker with a vast pool of potential support. If a filmmaker needs money quickly, individuals are the fastest source of support. Many individual donations are possible in a short amount of time. Also, this type of fundraising entails establishing a direct connection with the donor, and generally involves very little paperwork.

Downside: This type of fundraising is very labor-intensive. Donations generally trickle in over long periods of time, and arrive in small-to-medium amounts. Individual donations are usually in the hundreds of dollars (or less), occasionally in the thousands of dollars, and very rarely in the tens of thousands of dollars.

How Do I Find Them?

People with money for film and video projects are everywhere —
quite often in the most obvious places, the ones filmmakers might
take for granted. Here is a laundry list of places and methods for
finding individual donors:

◆ **In your head.** The filmmaker should take a moment to think
  about everyone he has ever met who likes him and/or might
  take an interest in his project. Rummage through memories
  of parties, past jobs, conversations with friends, business lun-
  cheons, and attendance at official receptions.

◆ **In your Rolodex.** The filmmaker should go through *every* name
  in his address book, Rolodex, or electronic organizing device and
  see if these generate any ideas or leads. Look at each and every
  name and ask: "Is this a person who could be of some help to me?
  Is this a person whom I should ask for support? Is this a person
  who might give me leads to other people or organizations?"

◆ **In your family.** Do not rule out asking close relatives and friends
  for support — they are often the first donors to a project. Keep
  in mind that the vast majority of individual donations come from
  people with annual incomes below $50,000. Filmmakers are
  often hesitant to ask friends and family, but if they are appropriate and if the filmmaker feels they can afford to help, then the
  task is to find a comfortable way to make an approach.

◆ **In your local newspaper.** Check out the appropriate sections
  of local and national newspapers for people who have shown
  interest in the topic area of the film (for documentaries), including the business pages and society columns. It is surprising how
  often newspapers list the causes supported by individuals, and
  even how much they gave.

◆ **Throw a brainstorming party.** A very effective way to garner
  names is to throw a brief evening gathering where the filmmaker asks guests to help brainstorm names of people and
  organizations that might contribute.

◆ **Cast out/into the Net.** The Internet is an excellent place to get
  word out about a filmmaker's project to niche groups and begin
  to find people of similar interests who might lend support. Look
  for appropriate blogs and Web sites by topic area and post notes

there if the Webmaster will allow it. Establish a Web site and/or blog of your own and have it linked to other sites where people might want to find you. Become involved in social networking sites (MySpace, Facebook, Twitter, etc.).

- **The Social Register** (available for a dozen major cities).
- **Membership and Donor Lists.** Check the back of annual reports, performance programs, and Web site donor lists from nonprofit organizations where target donors are likely to have already contributed. This is a rich source of information on potential donors. The lovely thing about these donor lists is that they almost always provide the amount of money each person gave — an important piece of information.
- *Who's Who.* Editions of *Who's Who* are available nationally and for regions, as well as various professions.

How to Approach Individuals

- **One-on-One (or Two-on-One).** This is a direct, in-person "ask" and is statistically the single most effective way to get money. The one-on-one ask may also be the most difficult one to arrange. A variant on this is the over-the-phone ask (only good with people you already know).
- **Fundraising Houseparty.** This is *not* to be confused with a fundraising event where you charge admission. A fundraising houseparty is one where a number of people are invited to an evening soiree at someone's home. Everyone invited understands that a presentation will be given that night about your film, and that participants will have a chance to decide about making a contribution. (For a very detailed description of this type of event, refer to my book, *The Fundraising Houseparty: How to Party with a Purpose and Raise Money for Your Cause — 2nd Edition* available at www.warshawski.com).
- **Direct Mail.** There are two variants for direct mail approaches.
  - The first is a **personal letter** sent by you to just a few people you know personally, or by an avid supporter who will write to his own friends.
  - The second is a **mass mail** appeal sent to a list you have acquired of possible supporters (members of clubs, organizations, magazine subscribers, etc.).

◆ **The Internet.** This area of fundraising has been growing exponentially in the last few years. E-mail letter appeals to individuals is one approach, but only if the recipient feels that the mailing is not a mass "spam" appeal. Linking your letter to a Web site and/or blog that has more details is a good idea. Listserves and social networking groups (like Facebook) are another way to get information out about your project and your need for support. Typically, this works best if the filmmaker has a cause-related program, and the notice is being sent by an organization that is involved in that cause and has a large membership list.

GOVERNMENT

Upside: When a government source awards a grant it is usually a substantial amount, in the thousands of dollars. Government grants are very easy to research, and agencies that reject you must provide you with feedback on your application if requested.

Downside: When the economy is down, government grants shrink considerably and become even more competitive than usual. Paperwork can be very extensive (long application, follow-up reports, and accounting). Some government agencies are very worried about political scrutiny, so controversial topics have a more difficult time finding support here.

How Do I Do the Research?

There are three levels of government support available: National, State, and Local.

Nationally, the major sources include:
- National Endowment for the Arts
- National Endowment for the Humanities
- Corporation for Public Broadcasting
- Public Broadcasting Service
- Miscellaneous government agencies (e.g. Forestry, IRS)

On the **State** level there are typically:
- State Arts Agencies
- State Humanities Councils
- State Tourism Boards

On the **Local** level there are very few agencies that give support, but you can look for:
- Local City or Regional Arts Council
- Local/Regional Commerce and Growth Associations
- City Tourism Board

Information on Government sources can be found through:
- **Catalog of Federal Domestic Assistance.** Available in most libraries.
- **Directly from the agencies themselves.** All publish their own guidelines and application forms and can be found on the Web.
- **Foundation Center Libraries.** Located in most metropolitan centers, these libraries are a great font of information. (See detailed note in next section).
- **Internet.** Every Federal agency, and many state and local agencies, maintain their own Web sites replete with information and, often, downloadable application forms.

How to Approach Government Agencies

Very simply: Get the guidelines, determine if you and the agency are a good match, request the application form and fill out as appropriate, and contact a program officer before sending in materials to cover any questions you might have.

PRIVATE FOUNDATIONS

Upside: In the last two decades private foundations experienced an explosion in the size of their endowments and the numbers in their ranks. Foundations with a variety of interests can be found throughout the U.S. Grants are almost always in the thousands of dollars, and foundations are very easy to research.

Downside: It takes a long time to finally see a dollar from a foundation, and often years of work setting the stage for an ask — six to eighteen months is not unusual. Some foundations meet only once or twice a year, so it is important to be very mindful of deadlines. Paperwork is usually extensive (introductory letter, full grant proposal, follow-up reports, and accounting). Competition for foundation support is always very stiff, and increases when the economy is in a slump.

How Do I Do the Research?

◆ **Foundation Center Libraries.** These are the first and best places to go. The Foundation Center Libraries contain many books that list foundations, their areas of interest, application procedures and grants they have given in the past, as well as basic books on how to write grants. The Foundation Center maintains cooperating center branches in every major city in the U.S. For the one closest to you call: 1 (800) 424-9836 or visit their Web site at *www.fdncenter.org.*
Their five main branches are as follows:
  • New York City, 79 Fifth Avenue, (212) 620-4230
  • San Francisco, 312 Sutter Street, (415) 397-0902
  • Washington, D.C., 1001 Connecticut Avenue, N.W., (202) 331-1400
  • Cleveland, 1422 Euclid, Suite 1356, (216) 861-1933
  • Atlanta, Suite 150, Hurt Bldg., 50 Hurt Plaza, (404) 880-0094

◆ **Local Public Library.** Most public libraries have all the basic texts. Two main texts are: *The Foundation Directory* and the *National Data Book of Foundations.*

◆ **Foundations themselves.** Once you have targeted a foundation, always request a copy of their latest annual report and guidelines for grant applications.

◆ **The Internet.** Most foundations maintain their own Web sites; you can discover a wealth of information right there. Often they list an e-mail contact for correspondence. More and more foundations are accepting electronic applications. Check out the Council on Foundation's Website (*www.cof.org*), which contains a wealth of information on its two thousand-plus members. Also, see the Bibliography for a list of Internet sources for doing research.

◆ **Fast Forward and Record.** Yes, watch PBS for any programs that are similar to yours (or rent them), then record the end credits that list all the funders! These are probably the same national and local foundations that will have an interest in your project.

♦ **Professional Journals.** Both in your topic area and in film/video. Watch for other projects and see where their funding is coming from.

♦ **Network.** Start going to as many places as you can where other filmmakers and people in your topic interest gather — parties, cafés, conferences, workshops. These gatherings offer great opportunities for up-to-date information on funding patterns.

How to Approach Foundations

After doing all the research possible and discovering everything there is to know about the foundation (and about your project), try to make an in-person meeting or at least a phone call with the appropriate program officer. If at all possible, avoid having to write an initial letter of inquiry before that personal contact — letters of inquiry make it too easy to be rejected. After that, complete whatever paperwork the foundation requests, which usually takes the form of a full written grant proposal.

CORPORATIONS

Upside: Corporations have many doors to walk through including:

- corporate foundation office
- the CEO or CFO office
- advertising and marketing departments
- community relations, public relations
- human resources
- employee-designated contributions

This is a good environment for entrepreneurial filmmakers. Contributions can be made rather quickly. Contributions can come in the form of money, goods, and/or services.

Downside: It is very hard to do research on corporate funding (at least for corporations without official foundations). Corporations are much more interested in "strategic investments" than in pure donations, so the filmmaker's project usually has to provide an advertising, public relations, or promotion benefit to the company. It helps tremendously to have a personal connection, or someone who will provide entrée.

How Do I Do the Research?

- **Foundation Records.** If a corporation has its own foundation, then you can follow the instructions for private foundations above.
- **Newspapers.** The other best source for information is the business section of your local newspaper (and national publications like the *Wall Street Journal*). The newspaper provides great leads on the current fiscal condition of companies. Do not approach a corporation, for instance, at the end of a very bad earnings quarter.
- *The Directory of International Corporate Giving in America* — available in most libraries.
- **Standard and Poor's** — *Register of Corporations, Directors and Executives.*
- **Magazines:** *Fortune* (see their annual "Fortune 500 List" issue, also available on their Web site), *Advertising Age, Forbes, INC, Fast Company.*
- **Internet.** Find the corporation's Web site and see if there is any information about applying for donations.
- **Annual Reports.** A good way to find out what the corporation is interested in, its fiscal viability, and whether or not it has a department concerned with community affairs.

How to Approach Corporations

For corporate foundations, use the same instructions as for private foundations. In all other instances, you will need to identify the right person in the right office first (e.g., CEO, Director of Marketing, Employee Contributions Representative). Be prepared to tell the corporation exactly how it will benefit from being associated with your project (this usually translates as a strong correlation between your audience and the demographics and/or psychographics of their customers). Provide whatever written materials they might request (sometimes a short letter with a budget, sometimes a full-blown detailed proposal).

SMALL BUSINESSES

Upside: They are everywhere and are very easy to approach. Little or no paperwork is involved, and there are rarely any reporting requirements. Contribution decision is made very quickly — in a matter of days or weeks. Little or no research is necessary.

Downside: Small businesses rarely give money. They are much more likely to provide donated goods and services (free pizzas for the crew, free use of cell phones, free photocopying). Donations are usually modest. Giving is often based on a strong community connection to the project.

How Do I Do the Research?

- ◆ **Chamber of Commerce.** Check for their list of members.
- ◆ *Business Journal.* Subscribe to or locate your city's edition.
- ◆ **Clubs and Associations.** Attend meetings of the local Rotary and Kiwanis Clubs.
- ◆ **Local Television.** Watch late night TV to see who advertises.
- ◆ **The Better Business Bureau** — a good place to check references.
- ◆ **Snoop.** Walk around your neighborhood. Make notes about local businesses and visit them to introduce yourself.
- ◆ *The Yellow Pages.* Let your fingers do the walking.

How to Approach Small Businesses

The personal approach works best. Contact the business by phone or in person to find out who to "ask," and be prepared to hand over a short document with:

- • A very brief description of the project with information on your crew.
- • The benefit to the donor. This could be in the form of free publicity through a credit in the film and/or on its packaging, free copies of the program, or an invitation to a local premiere where the business will be thanked in public.
- • The types of goods/services you are requesting (e.g., three free lunches for a crew of ten, twenty copies of a sixty-page script).
- • Local references.

OTHER NONPROFITS

Upside: There are some niche pots of money available from organizations and agencies in increasing numbers. Often these are very localized and emphasize a larger number of small grants.

Downside: No long tradition of funding, so research can be difficult, especially as new sources crop up.

How Do I Do the Research?

Ear-to-the-ground, plus all other methods recommended above. In this arena, professional journals are a key source of information. Some agencies that fit in this category include:

- Religious Denominations
- United Way
- Independent Television Service-ITVS (an agency under the wing of the Corporation for Public Broadcasting)
- Foreign television stations (e.g., Channel Four in Britain, Canal+ in France, ZDF in Germany) who are interested in co-productions
- Foreign governments with grants for co-productions that take place primarily on their soil and/or with local talent
- Fraternities and sororities
- VFW, Knights of Columbus, Lions Club, Rotary International

How to Approach Other Nonprofits

The approach will vary in this arena from donor to donor, so there are no pat rules. Foreign entities, for instance, almost always will need to be contacted in person, which makes this type of funding very difficult. ITVS has printed guidelines available on its Web site (www.itvs.org). ITVS has become a key source of funding for independent projects of an alternative nature intended for television. You will find a sample ITVS grant proposal at the end of the book. Churches and other nonprofits will need to be researched and approached on a case-by-case basis. Nonprofit service organizations might make an outright donation, or want to make pre-buys of your program as benefits to their members and/or for fundraising purposes.

MIXING IT UP

Once the filmmaker has a grasp of the full universe of potential support, the next question is "What mix of fundraising support is the best for me and my project?" A fundraising plan has to be created because no one has the time and the energy necessary to pursue all avenues of possible support. There are some quick guidelines that can help the filmmaker with this issue. The first is to realize that some projects are just more naturally appropriate for some types of support. The second filter is to realize that some filmmakers are more naturally predisposed and skillful at certain types of approaches — these filmmakers are great schmoozers, or wonderful grant writers, or great at working with community members.

With regard to the right "fit" for your project with funders, here is a loose overview:

- **Documentaries.** Social issue documentaries enjoy the broadest possible avenues of support — appropriate for almost every type of fundraising.
- **Independent dramatic features and shorts.** Best bets are individuals approached one-on-one or in fundraising houseparty settings. Occasionally noncommercial features can find grant support from foundations and government agencies, but usually only if there is a social issue involved. Corporate support might be forthcoming if there is product or audience crossover within the interests of the business.
- **Experimental or "personal" work.** Video art and experimental films have very limited avenues of support — just a handful of private foundations and a few government agencies. These works rarely receive support from corporations or small businesses. Individuals can be a good source of support, but there usually has to be an already established connection between the filmmaker and the donor.
- **Animated films.** Very few funders are interested in animation as an art form. If the animated film has any type of "message" or can be used in an educational setting, then funding can be found through all appropriate channels. If the animated work is primarily entertaining and/or personal or experimental in

nature, then the filmmaker can look to a few government and private foundations, and perhaps individuals.

Later in this book I will be discussing in more detail the specifics of making each approach more effective. This will help the filmmaker decide which approaches are more suited to her skills, her project, and her resources (time, money, and volunteer support). For instance, the documentary filmmaker might end up deciding that for her one-hour program she will try to pursue the following mix of support:

- 50% from three or four private foundations
- 20% from state humanities councils
- 15% from four fundraising houseparties
- 15% from individuals through an Internet letter-writing campaign

Whatever mix chosen, try to pick one that has a high probability of success for you and the project. Sooner or later the filmmaker will have to present this fundraising "plan" to potential donors who will want to feel that it is plausible. More important, sooner or later the filmmaker will actually have to traverse this road toward a goal of adequately funding a project.

FOR-PROFIT

The one area of fundraising that I do not cover in this book is the whole world of for-profit investments — support that comes to your project but is not a tax-deductible charitable donation. These major sources include:

- ◆ **International Pre-Sales**: Usually brokered by an International Sales Agent/Company. A good place to research what foreign broadcasters are looking for is the annual European Documentary Network's *Financing Guide* (www.edn.dk).
- ◆ **Gap and Supergap financing**: Typically, a bank loan in the amount of 10% – 30% of the film's budget.
- ◆ **Federal and State tax incentives**: These are offered federally and on a state-by-state basis and can change annually. There are professionals who specialize in assisting with this.

- **Deferments:** If your project does indeed look like it can make a profit, it is not unusual for the producer and/or cast members to defer all or part of their fees (usually to be recouped ahead of all other financing).
- **Equity Investors:** This can be single or multi-source and you'll need a good lawyer to put together all the appropriate paperwork. The rules for how you can approach and involve equity investors vary from state-to-state.
- **Postproduction House Investor:** Sometimes you can get a postproduction house to "invest" part or all of its services.
- **Sponsorship and Product Placement:** A sponsorship involves providing logo exposure outside of the film for a company, and product placement entails featuring the product directly in the film.

To pursue most of these you will need a good entertainment attorney and/or accountant. More and more filmmakers are mixing nonprofit and for-profit sources of support. Innes Smolansky is a lawyer who has worked with many independent filmmakers. As she notes: "Traditionally, independent feature films were funded with investments or loans and independent documentaries were funded with grants and donations. Today we see more and more combinations of the two types of funding in the same project." Here is Innes' simple road map to keeping your options open for different kinds of funding:

ROAD MAP TO MIXING
DONATIONS & INVESTMENTS

- **Incorporate.** A limited liability company (LLC) is considered to be the most popular and convenient legal structure through which to fundraise and produce a film. While other for-profit structures may be considered, creating and producing a film through a not-for-profit 501(c)(3) corporation will limit your ability to attract both investments and donations for the same project.
- **Create a Budget.** Before you start fundraising, have a clear understanding of your budget needs. Have a Best Case Scenario Budget and a Worst Case Scenario Budget.
- **Identify Your Funding Options.** This is often an ongoing process, but try to identify the big categories, for example: private loans and equity investments from friends, family and co-producing partners; donations from private individuals and grants from various granting organizations; pre-sale of some media rights, etc. Except for donations, all the funds that you raise should go directly into your LLC, but to receive donations you need a Fiscal Sponsor.
- **Find the "Right" Fiscal Sponsor.** You should identify a not-for-profit 501(c)(3) organization that has a logical connection with your project. This usually means that one of the purposes of a fiscal sponsor's existence must be to support audiovisual projects, or a cause that your film falls under.
- **Channel the Funds.** All the funds you raise as donations from private individuals or grants that require a 501(c)(3) organization to receive them should be channeled through your fiscal sponsor. The donor or granting organization should send the funds directly to the fiscal sponsor, clearly identifying for which project the funds are to be used. The fiscal sponsor will deduct an administration fee (usually between 5% and 12%), and transmit the rest to your LLC. The donor will receive a receipt from the fiscal sponsor for making a tax-deductible charitable donation. You can then use the funds received from the fiscal sponsor for production of your film and keep your portion of the profits should your film turn out to be profitable.

— Innes Smolansky, Esq.
innes@filmlegal.com

CHAPTER THREE

PATCHWORK QUILT —
Putting Your
Project Together

"You don't have to plan to fail.
You just have to fail to plan."
— Author Unknown

Filmmakers who come to me for advice have usually "hit the wall" in fundraising — they have tried everything possible to acquire support for a project but just can't seem to get past a certain point. I am often placed in the position of having to determine and then tell filmmakers what they are doing wrong so we can understand why their rate of rejection is so high. I said earlier that many fundraising problems are rooted in basic career development issues (e.g. comportment, mission, professional direction). There is one other great impediment to funding: hitting the street before the filmmaker is actually ready to fully articulate the project in a logically convincing and emotionally engaging manner.

THE STORY THAT HAD TO BE TOLD

What the filmmaker must ask before beginning to fundraise is: "Do I know everything I must know about this project before I approach a funder? Can I answer any potential questions about my project that anyone might ask?" Too many filmmakers start looking for money before they have done the very basic groundwork on their project, and this lack of preparation leads to a number of quick rejections by potential funders. When I ask filmmakers how they got involved with projects, they often say, "I ran across this incredible story/person/organization and I knew immediately that this was a story that must be told." I have heard this sentence almost word-for-word so often that it must be a virus specific to independent filmmakers.

What I have never heard a filmmaker say is, "This is a story that must be heard." In other words, the filmmaker must realize that just because the idea for the film fills her with great excitement and she feels an overwhelming compulsion to tell it, she must prove that a lot of other people will feel the same way and want to hear her story. She will have to fully address basic questions of need, audience, distribution, marketing, crew and staff, and budget. Until these are all as well articulated as possible, it is a mistake to start looking for financial support.

Question Number One concerns "need." Is there a need in the world for one more film about XYZ? I ask my clients the following questions: "Can you name five titles of other films that people will think of immediately when you mention your new film?" If the filmmaker says "no," then I know more homework needs to be done.

Every film fits into some niche where it will be clustered with other similar titles or subjects. The filmmaker has to do the research that uncovers all these films. When any seem very close in content, the filmmaker must make an effort to actually see those films. No funder wants to place support behind a program that has already been made by another filmmaker. There are many ways to uncover the titles of your "competition": filmographies available in libraries, catalogs from distributors of films in your genre or subject area, conversations with experts in the field, lists of programs aired on PBS, and the Internet Movie Database (*www.imdb.com*).

Keep in mind that when you make your initial pitch to funders, whether or not they articulate it out loud, they will be thinking, "I know another film or two that's about the exact same subject — how is this any different?" The filmmaker must be ready to *differentiate* her project from all others that have already been created. She has to be ready to say, "My program is different from all others in the following ways...".

Here are some areas where a filmmaker can make a case for significant differentiation from another similar project:

- **Timing:** The project is much more current than anything previously created, and contains brand new information.
- **Depth:** The project is longer and goes into much more depth on the subject than any other previous film.
- **Content:** The project covers issues and aspects of the topic that have never been covered before and/or from a different perspective.
- **Style:** The project will be the first animated/narrative/vérité documentary on the subject ever made.
- **Audience:** the project will be made for a particular audience (the elderly, young children, illegal immigrants) that has never had access to this information.

The idea is a very simple and basic one: *Make sure the project is significantly different from anything else currently available.* Be able to convince potential donors that there is a genuine need in the world for this film, because it has something important to say in a way that hasn't been heard before. When I cover the elements of the perfect written proposal, I will be advising the inclusion of a whole section on this topic in the grant.

One important principle to remember when differentiating your project from others is to *never say anything negative about other films and/or filmmakers.* It is a mistake to differentiate the program by saying "My film will be better than the others because they are all substandard works of filmmaking, and mine will be a beautiful and professional work of art." Even if this is true, saying this only places the filmmaker in an unflattering light.

AUDIENCE/ COMMUNITY

Sooner or later the filmmaker wants the work to reach an audience. Deciding who that audience will be is something that should happen as early in the project as possible. If I ask a filmmaker who her audience is, I usually get the following answer: "Everybody!"

Unfortunately, not only is this answer inaccurate and implausible (no film ever made could possibly appeal to everyone), this answer will not please funders, and it keeps the filmmaker from creating a program that is likely to really appeal to specific segments of the population.

Whom does the filmmaker want to reach? What types of people are most likely to be interested in the project? Among whom does the filmmaker want to make an impact?

Start by trying to draw circles of broad audience types, including but not limited to:

◆ Geography
◆ Age
◆ Race
◆ Gender
◆ Sex
◆ Sexual Orientation
◆ Religion
◆ Lifestyles, Hobbies, Leisure Interests
◆ Occupation
◆ Income Level
◆ Educational Background
◆ Political Affiliation

The filmmaker can begin to define the particular demographics and psychographics that make up the audience to be reached. For instance, a documentary might be geared to upper-middle-class women over thirty who live in urban environments throughout the U.S. and who are at a high risk for breast cancer, or the film might be targeted to young black males between the ages of thirteen and eighteen who come from single parent households.

There are important lessons to be learned from this exercise. The first is that the program's content and format might need adjusting so that it is better suited to the correct audience. Another lesson might be that the intended audience cannot afford the program, so funds for distribution will have to be added to the fundraising budget. The filmmaker should consider if this list has already begun to lead to ideas for finding support (e.g., prominent individuals and affinity organizations).

For the filmmaker who sincerely believes her film is being made for everybody, I suggest a process of elimination — a *reductio ad absurdum*. Start making lists of just the narrowest audience types imaginable who would in no way be interested in the film: Bedouin nomads, children under six, people who belong to religions that forbid watching television or movies. Eventually this process will help the filmmaker to back in to the audience.

Occasionally a filmmaker might embark on a project and actually not know who the potential audience is; the filmmaker only knows that the topic is compelling and that somebody out there must want to see it. In that case, I advise creating a process to start *finding* the audience as early in the process as possible — ideally well before the project reaches completion. This can be done in any number of creative ways, including:

- holding works-in-progress screenings with different focus groups
- circulating the treatment or script to people the filmmaker trusts
- consulting with experts in the subject area of the film
- talking to distributors and exhibitors
- social networking on the Web (blogs, special interest Web sites, MySpace, Facebook, etc.)

It will be very difficult to get funding support from sophisticated funders until the filmmakers can articulate just who she hopes to reach.

Here is an example of how the Web and blogs can help you find your audience:

> When Curt Ellis began working on *King Corn*, a documentary about the role that corn plays in the American diet and economy, he wasn't sure who the film's core audience was. Ellis was a co-producer and co-star of the movie, in which he and his friend Ian Cheney move to Iowa to grow an acre of corn. Ellis' cousin, Aaron Woolf, was the film's director.
>
> "They always tell you, 'Think about your audience from Day One, before you ever pick up a camera,'" Ellis says. "We weren't. We were busy trying to figure out how

to tell a really complicated story in a way that'd be relevant and interesting for our audience — whoever they turned out to be."

But along the way, as Ellis and his collaborators began to conduct interviews, people introduced them to groups like Slow Food International, foundations dealing with agricultural and dietary issues and bloggers writing about sustainability and the environment.

"We realized that all those people are naturally interested in our film, and started connecting with that built-in audience," Ellis says. Some bloggers, he says, suggested people who'd make good interviewees — or who might provide a promotional boost to the film when it was ready.

— From an ITVS case study of *King Corn* by Scott Kirsner, *www.itvs.org* (reprinted with permission)

More and more, funders are interested in the "community" you plan to reach — how you plan to create a community around your film. Here is what Todd Dagres, producer (*Transiberian*) and venture capitalist, had to say about this subject at a recent DIY Days Conference in Boston:

"The key to success producing content for the new medium, the digital web, is 'community.' If you're a traditional TV or film person... you think of 'audience,' you think 'I've got to make something that this demographic wants to see.' You're already deciding that you're in a passive medium, and you're already deciding that you want somebody to watch this and then go home, or watch this and then go someplace else. So you're building an 'audience.' Forget the word 'audience.' The new word is 'community'... you have to build a community around the content. In fact the content is nothing but a seed to build that community. The community interacts with content."

DISTRIBUTION

Once the question of need is answered, and the target audiences have been identified, the next piece of the puzzle is distribution — how the filmmaker intends to get the completed program out to the world. This has become a central concern for funders. They are well aware of one of the sad facts of life in independent filmmaking: Many films are made, but few are seen by their full intended audience.

This is why it is smart to talk to bona fide distributors very early in the process of your thinking about and creating a project. Distributors are a great font of practical, real-world information on the potential for marketing a program and making sure it reaches viewers. Begin the process of identifying the perfect distributors of the film being made. There are lists of distributors of independent film and video programs that can be found on the Internet. Catalogs are often available in libraries and in institutions that purchase media products. Check to see who distributes the other films that you consider to be your competition. Other filmmakers are also a great source of advice about distributors.

I recommend doing some homework on distributors that are appropriate for your current and future projects, and then picking up a phone and calling them directly for a conversation (perhaps preceded by an introductory e-mail). What questions can be asked of a distributor at this early state in a project?

- Is there a need for my project in the marketplace?
- Is the project the right length and format for the audience?
- What is the potential for sales in dollars and units over what length of time?
- Are other similar projects in the pipeline?
- Does this program have to have a study guide and/or a Web site?

If the distributor is enthusiastic about the project, be sure to ask for a letter of support — this is the most credible evidence that can be given to a funder to help prove the eventual viability of a program. Get these letters whenever possible.

I had a client once who was creating a three-hour series for grade school children on the environment. He called a distributor who was very excited by the idea because it had not been done before and teachers were making requests for anything he might have on the topic. The filmmaker was ecstatic, until the distributor told him the following: "I love your idea, but I can't take your series." The filmmaker wanted to know why. The distributor answered, "Because you're making three one-hour films. In my market, teachers want either twenty-minute or thirty-minute films." Now the filmmaker knew that if he could cut his work to have natural twenty or thirty-minute sections he would have a much better chance at reaching his audience. Imagine how expensive this lesson would have been had he waited until after completing his three-hour series to talk to a distributor.

The filmmaker will have to resolve the entire landscape of the eventual distribution of the program. What markets will the program explore and in what sequence? Broadly, the markets include:

- Festivals
- Theatrical
- Cable Television (Pay-Per-View, Premium Channels, Basic Cable, Public Access)
- Public Television (national and local)
- Commercial Broadcast Television
- Home Video
- Educational Markets
- Organizations, Associations, and Libraries
- Catalogs
- The Internet
- Domestic and International outlets for all of the above

Do not make the mistake of telling a funder that the sole intended distribution outlet is PBS. Funders want to see a distribution plan that is much more rich and varied than just public television. Increasingly, funders are also interested in knowing about specific marketing/public relations plans, community outreach plans, and whether or not a Web site and/or blog will be created in conjunction with the film.

I like to ask funders about their pet peeves. One funder confided the following to me: "If a filmmaker tells me that her only method of distribution will be a PBS broadcast, then I won't fund her. I need to hear a distribution plan that is much more varied and multifarious than just PBS, otherwise I can't make the grant."

Peter Broderick, President of Paradigm Consulting, specializes in helping filmmakers and media companies develop strategies to maximize distribution, audience, and revenues. Here is a short case study where he describes that new nexus between audience/community and distribution for the documentary *Note by Note*:

TARGETING CORE AUDIENCES

Today independent filmmakers are taking a new approach to audience. While studios continue to spend vast amounts of money chasing general audiences, independents are learning to target core audiences successfully. They are implementing strategies designed to reach the specific audiences most likely to be interested in their films. Documentary filmmakers have been particularly effective connecting with viewers interested in the subject of their films.

Note by Note is an irresistible documentary about the making of a Steinway piano. The most thoroughly handcrafted instruments in the world, Steinway pianos are as unique and full of personality as the world-class musicians who play them. Ben Niles, the film's director, made a major effort to define and reach the film's core audiences, which include Steinway dealers, Steinway owners, piano students and their parents, piano teachers, piano technicians, pianists, and many others.

NOTE BY NOTE ECOSYSTEM

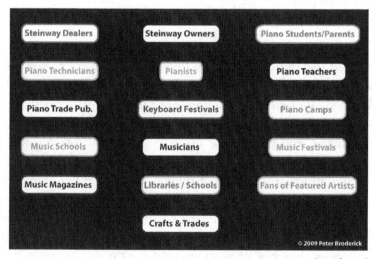

(*continues*)

TARGETING CORE AUDIENCES (cont.)

Ben's priority was to first reach these core audiences, and then hopefully cross over to a wider public. He is reaching them both online and offline through his Web site, mailing list, organizational partnerships, and publications read by his audiences.

After winning awards and acclaim on the festival circuit, *Note by Note* opened theatrically at the Film Forum in New York City where it was a box office and critical success. Working with Argot Pictures, the filmmaker opened the film across the country, mixing regular theatrical engagements with single-night special event screenings. At a number of these screenings, it was possible to not only watch the film but also meet the main character, Steinway #L1037, and hear it played before or after the film. These special event screenings were particularly popular, selling out in many cities and extending the semi-theatrical life of the film for over a year.

Niles has been successfully selling DVDs at screenings and from his website, *www.notebynotethemovie.com*. In late 2009, the film will be broadcast nationally and be released in video stores around the country and online.

Most filmmakers who have effectively targeted core audiences begin with an initial idea of which viewers will be most interested in their films and then discover new audiences along the way. Independents willing to put the time and effort into a core audience strategy, are much more likely to get their films seen widely and to maximize revenues.

For more information on hybrid distribution to core audiences, visit *www.peterbroderick.com*.

GOOD COMPANY

The crew that works on the film can be a defining factor in whether or not a funder feels comfortable investing their funds in a project. The first thing to decide is what role you, the filmmaker, will play in the project — writer, director, producer, cinematographer, editor. Next, the filmmaker must decide who will make up the rest of the team. There are very few formulas for fundraising success that I will give in this book. Almost all fundraising is a vast gray area with very little black-and-white clarity, because so many things depend on the specific project and the filmmaker. However, there is one rule that applies to all projects looking for donations:

*The less experienced the filmmaker, the more expe-
rienced the crew must be. The more experienced the
filmmaker, the less experienced the crew needs to be.*

The issue here is very simply one of credibility. Generally,
funders are more comfortable dealing with filmmakers that have
a proven track record. Emerging filmmakers doing their first or
second program, and who have not raised large amounts of money
before or earned any critical accolades or awards, are at a distinct
disadvantage. They are still climbing that steep hill of credibility. In
those instances, I tell the filmmaker to attach experienced people to
their projects in key roles. I also highly recommend finding someone
with an excellent reputation to act as an advisor to the project. Get
that person to write a letter that says he agrees to make available
a certain number of hours or days at a certain rate of pay, during
which he will provide assistance to the project. I have seen many
young filmmakers have success fundraising because they were able
to attach well-known artists to their projects.

I told this once to an emerging filmmaker who had an ambitious
project on the drawing board. I asked what filmmakers she respected
most. One name popped up immediately: a filmmaker with a long
history of creating excellent ethnographic documentaries. As it happens, I knew that this filmmaker lived in her city and was listed in the
phonebook, so I encouraged her to give him a call. She was frightened
about the prospect of a "cold call" so we did a quick role-play. Then
she made the phone call and, miraculously, the filmmaker answered
the phone himself. They had a great conversation, he invited her to
have lunch with him, and soon he had signed a letter of agreement
to serve as an official advisor to the project. The filmmaker wrote his
day rate into her budget, attached his letter of commitment to all her
grant proposals, and it made a significant difference in boosting her
credibility and acquiring funds for her project.

GOOD TIMING

Funders are also going to want to know how long it will take to
complete the program. Unfortunately, a true answer is usually,
"Longer than I promised!" Films almost always take longer to complete than initially promised. The main reason is that fundraising

is unpredictable and never comes together as quickly or as easily as we would like. The filmmaker needs to step back and begin to think about the long-term implications of embarking on a noncommercial film project. If everything goes as planned, the entire process — from thinking of the idea, through fundraising, production, post-production and entering distribution — might take as little as three years. Most of my clients would consider this a speedy schedule. However, ambitious projects that entail large sums of money might take much longer. Even small projects about difficult subject matter can also take much longer. It is not at all unusual for a project to eat up five or more years of a filmmaker's life.

What must be presented to funders is a timeline for the entire project that shows a good-faith estimate for how long all the various parts of the project would take from conception all the way through the beginning of distribution, if there were no unusual interruptions. It is much smarter to overestimate the time than to underestimate. I often tell clients it is going to take 50% more time to do the project than they predict.

A typical timeline should be generic in terms of years/months and not chronologically specific. In other words, never say "I will begin research on June 1, and go into production on August 28, then edit the program in December." What invariably happens is that as the project progresses all these dates get changed. It is much better to show all elements in blocks of time. Here is a sample of a simple generic timeline.

	YEAR ONE				YEAR TWO				YEAR THREE			
QUARTER	1st	2nd	3rd	4th	1st	2nd	3rd	4th	1st	2nd	3rd	4th
ACTIVITY												
Research	x											
Fundraising	x	x	x	x	x	x	x	x	x			
Script Writing			x									
Preproduction				x	x							
Production						x	x					
Postproduction								x	x	x		
Distribution											x->	

With this timeline in hand, the filmmaker can say to the funder, "This is how long each aspect of my project will take, and how long the entire effort will go, if there are no interruptions and if fundraising moves smoothly."

MONEY MATTERS

Budgeting, like distribution, is a science in and of itself. There are whole books written on these topics, and I recommend reading them if these areas are new to a filmmaker. What I have found with budgets is that they are accurate mirrors of most things that are either right or wrong with a project. I often read a project budget before I look at the narrative description. When I read a budget I am looking for a story. Too often I find myself reading a mystery, a comedy, or a horror story, when what I am looking for is a good romance.

After determining all the other elements of a project it is time to sit down and create a fiscal representation of what it will take to make the filmmaker's dream a reality. This exercise must be done on a computer using some type of spreadsheet program, and not on a calculator, or using a pencil and accounting paper. Why? Because in filmmaking as in life, *things change*. This may be truer in filmmaking than in most other art forms because of the length of time involved to create new work. In any event, the only environment for budget forecasting that is amenable to change is a spreadsheet where you can change one or two figures in a very complicated budget and have everything else change instantaneously.

To begin a project, consider creating two different budgets. Budget Number One is the "Best Case Scenario Budget." For this budget, figure out reasonable cash costs for everything you need to create the project in just the way that would make it a perfect program that meets a certain set of standards. This will be the budget that is used to begin fundraising and will be shown to potential funders in one form or another throughout the process.

Budget Number Two is the "Worst Case Scenario Budget." This budget is more important than the first, but it will never be shown to anyone. It is the budget that is kept in a drawer and only pulled out when the filmmaker "hits the wall," is finally fed up with fundraising, and just wants to finish up as soon as possible. For this budget, go through every item in the detailed Best Case Scenario asking "How can I eliminate, reduce, beg, borrow, or steal items to make this budget as small as possible *but still create a program of which I am proud?*" A filmmaker should never cross over a line of minimum standard and self-respect. But generally there is quite a bit of wiggle room between the ideal budget and one that is more livable. After the minimum amount has been reached in fundraising, the filmmaker will have to assess whether or not the effort needed to raise more funds is worth the value added to the program.

The entire budget can be built around a simple grid showing for each budget item: Number, Frequency, Cost Basis, Total. Later as things get more complicated, "Total" will be divided up into two separate columns showing "Cash" and "In-Kind." An in-kind contribution is one where someone is providing either a service or some goods as a donation and is not asking for a cash payment. For instance, a lab might provide $10,000 worth of services at a 30% discount — so the budget would show $7,000 cash, $3,000 in-kind and a total of $10.000. Still later, when the project is off and rolling, the filmmaker is going to add yet another subdivided column that shows "$ Raised To-Date" and "$ Still Needed."

Get in the habit of adding notes to any and all budget items that might eventually draw a question from a funder. Be liberal with these notes as they will help with funders who are inexperienced reading film budgets. Most funders will accept an unusually high cost for an item if there is a good reason for it. For instance, I worked once with filmmakers who showed a twenty-to-one shooting ratio, which was going to mean very high film stock costs and extra processing expenses. Their reasoning was that they would be shooting in a part of the world where they would not have access to film stock if they ran out, and where they had only one chance to shoot and get it right. They wrote this explanation as a note directly on their budget and funders had no problem accepting the expense as being valid.

In general, here are some basic tips and notes for noncommercial film project budgets:

◆ **Fair and Comparable.** The simple rule of thumb for deciding what to pay for any item on the budget is whatever is *fair and comparable for the experience of the person doing the work, the type of work being done, and the city where the work takes place.*

For many types of work and for many types of purchases, fair and comparable will vary widely from one location to another.

◆ **Pay Yourself!** Funders are suspicious of budgets that show the filmmaker paying herself nothing. It makes the filmmaker very suspect in the eyes of the funder. Filmmakers must begin budgets assuming that some fair level of payment will be coming to them, even if they know in their bones that they are ready to donate time when needed if it will help complete the project.

◆ **Red Flags.** Go through the budget line by line and identify every item that might raise a red flag, then write an explanatory note.

◆ **Contingency.** A contingency is a percentage that is often added to film costs in case the film goes over budget. It is a safety net that almost every film needs, and is common in commercial budgets. However, in the nonprofit world, only include contingencies at the end of a budget when the funder has specifically said they would allow a contingency, or when the funder is very familiar with supporting film projects. Otherwise, it is best to not include any contingency at all. Funders unfamiliar with filmmaking will look at the contingency and immediately dismiss it, saying to themselves, "If I give the filmmaker money for a contingency she will definitely spend it, and if I don't she can probably finish the film for the lesser amount." So, my best advice is decide on a contingency percentage that feels fair and comfortable for the project, and then go ahead and factor it in to each item as you do the budget.

◆ **In-Kind Donations.** Most funders do not like to support projects that show a very high percentage of in-kind donations as part of the total budget. There are a couple of situations where in-kind donations are helpful. The first is early in the fundraising for a project, at its beginning stages when not much cash has yet been donated. Having commitments for in-kind donations from businesses and individuals shows that the project has some support and is being taken seriously. Another type of project where a high level of in-kind support is acceptable is a modestly budgeted project that is community-based, where free labor and the donation of goods can make a tremendous difference.

◆ **Equipment Purchase.** Rarely will a foundation allow its funds to be used for the purchase of equipment. I would avoid ever including the purchase of equipment in a budget, even if the lease/rental amount exceeds the price of purchase. By the way, if the filmmaker happens to already own a piece of equipment being used in a production, then it is fair to include a comparable rate of rental in the budget.

◆ **Distribution.** At the end of the budget, be sure to include funds to begin a distribution and community outreach effort. Some costs that can be listed are: Production Stills, Press Packets, DVD Copies, Graphic Design Fee, Festival Entry Fees, Web Site Design and Maintenance. If the film is going to the non-theatrical educational market, then funds for a teacher's guide should be added.

NONPROFIT – A DEFINITION

In this book I deal only with how filmmakers can convince donors to give money to projects that are inherently noncommercial in nature. The filmmaker needs to make a very basic decision upon embarking on a project. Is the film primarily a noncommercial effort that might accidentally have a commercial life, or is it a project from which the filmmaker fully hopes and intends to make a profit? There are no laws that limit a project that begins in the nonprofit world from going ahead to make a profit once it enters distribution. And there are no laws that preclude a project from receiving both tax-deductible charitable contributions from donors and investment dollars from investors.

I once served as Executive Producer on a feature (*The Stand-In*) starring the then little-known actor Danny Glover. When we ran out of our funds from the Rockefeller Foundation, the director turned to a friend of his for finishing funds in the form of an investment, which was repaid when we sold the home video rights. Some other grant-supported independent films that have gone on to make a profit include Spike Lee's first feature, *She's Gotta Have It*, and *Hoop Dreams*.

If the film in question is truly being made for educational purposes where the intent is more one of good conscience than profit, then the project is probably best off staying in the world of nonprofit donations and grants. If the project is clearly being made in order to recoup investment and create a profit, then it is better off staying in the commercial arena and looking for loans and/or investments. Filmmakers seeking investments will need to prepare a Private Placement Memorandum and comply with securities law — issues not covered in this book.

I recommend a simple test for deciding if a project that has a noncommercial intent should truly stay in that world or perhaps cross over into the world of commercial financing. I bring this up because if this route — investments — is open to the film, it can sometimes be an easier road to follow than the path of looking for grants and donations. My test entails doing the following:

- Calculate the total expense of producing the film and placing it into distribution.
- Next, create three income scenarios from all the possible distribution markets that you enumerated earlier — best case, middle case, and worst case.
- Go to your worst case income total and deduct from it your total expenses.

If the calculation shows a profit, or comes up close to being even, then save yourself a whole lot of time and trouble by forgetting about donations. Take out a loan, use a credit card, or find a few investors.

YOUR UMBRELLA – THE FISCAL SPONSOR

Let me be clear about the distinction between a donor and an investor. A donor is someone (or some agency) that is willing to donate money, goods, or services to a project without expecting any money back in return. An investor is someone who, when placing money, goods, or services into a project, expects a financial return on that "investment" under certain conditions. The investor wants a piece of the action. The donor wants only a receipt for a tax-deductible charitable donation plus the knowledge that something important will be created to help make the world a better place. This is a bit of a simplification, but the basic outline holds true.

The important wrinkle for an independent filmmaker is that in order for a donor to receive credit for a tax-deductible charitable donation, that donation must be given to a bona fide nonprofit organization — known by the IRS classification as a 501(c)(3). The filmmaker therefore has two choices:

1. Create her very own 501(c)(3) organization.
2. Find a Fiscal Sponsor — another nonprofit organization that already has 501(c)(3) status.

Opinions are split on which of these two routes is best. Generally, if the filmmaker has plans of making many noncommercial programs with substantial budgets over many years, then creating a nonprofit entity makes sense. The downside to this route is that it takes time to file the paperwork and receive nonprofit status from the IRS (eight months to a year is normal), and once the entity is created the filmmaker will need to file annual papers plus create a Board of Trustees who have ultimate legal control. There are a number of books that provide great advice on this process. The assistance of a lawyer will be necessary and this can be quite expensive unless the legal assistance is partially or totally *pro bono*. Sometimes a local chapter of the national organization called Volunteer Lawyers for the Arts can be of some initial help.

Otherwise, it is very easy for a filmmaker to find a Fiscal Sponsor to serve as the umbrella for the project. Who can be a fiscal sponsor? Any organization that already has nonprofit status. These include media arts centers, hospitals, schools, or associations. Some well-known fiscal sponsors for filmmakers include:

◆ Bay Area Video Coalition, and San Francisco Film Society (San Francisco)
◆ Center for Independent Documentary, Filmmakers' Collaborative, and Documentary Educational Resources (Boston)
◆ Chicago Filmmakers (Chicago)
◆ From the Heart Productions, and International Documentary Association (Los Angeles)
◆ New York Foundation for the Arts, Arts Engine, and Women Make Movies (New York)
◆ Southern Documentary Fund (North Carolina)

At the simplest level, the sponsor will accept checks for your project (e.g., the donor writes the check made out to the fiscal sponsor with your project as the beneficiary in the "note" or "for" section at the bottom of the check). Then the fiscal sponsor deposits that check and returns most or all of that money back to the filmmaker. Fiscal Sponsors and filmmakers negotiate what percentage will be kept by the umbrella organization for this service. An average range is currently between 5% and 10% — although I have seen some filmmakers negotiate a 0% fee, and I have also seen charges as high as 60%! A fiscal sponsor can do much more than just be a conduit for funds. The sponsor might also provide accounting services, advice about fundraising, connections with donors, and give office space and use of equipment.

Follow some basic common sense guidelines when setting up an arrangement with a fiscal sponsor:

- Pick a fiscal sponsor who is trustworthy and who sincerely appreciates you and the worth of the film being made.
- Demand that there be a written legal agreement.
- Make it clear that the filmmaker is the sole owner of copyright (e.g., this is not a "work for hire").
- Make it clear that the fiscal sponsor has no creative control of the project.
- Enumerate exactly how funds will be deposited, what happens to any earned interest, and under what schedule the filmmaker will receive payments once donations are made.

Once the agreement is sealed, have the sponsor write a very strong letter of support addressed "To Whom It May Concern" in which the sponsor gives the reasons for wanting to help with this project, and which urges other to help provide support. Also, get a copy of the sponsor's official letter from the IRS giving it nonprofit status. Both documents will be needed as fundraising progresses.

One last note about fiscal sponsors: *A project can have more that one fiscal sponsor.* This is important for projects that take place in more than one state and might need local sponsors to get donations from foundations or agencies that cannot donate out of their state. It is not unusual to receive donations from a couple of state humanities councils, for instance, that might have to write checks to entities within their state boundaries. Just make sure your agreements with fiscal sponsors are non-exclusive and that everyone knows who is on board.

Now let's finally hit the streets and start looking for money!

CHAPTER FOUR

GETTING PERSONAL —
Individual Donors

> *"The few projects in my study that disintegrated*
> *did so because the manager failed to build*
> *a coalition of supporters and collaborators."*
> *— Rosabeth Moss Kanter* (The Change Masters)

arlier I outlined the basic methods for identifying individuals who might contribute to a project, and the approaches that are appropriate for this type of fundraising. This chapter will take a closer and more detailed look at the nuts and bolts of this particular fundraising path.

If it is true that the vast majority of all the donations that go to all nonprofit endeavors in the U.S. come from individuals, why is it that more filmmakers do not pursue this path? I would suggest there are reasons external to the filmmaker, and there are internal barriers as well. One external reason might be that individual donors tend not to provide large donations. By "large" I mean in the tens of thousands of dollars. For a project that is looking for hundreds of thousands of dollars in support, it might not be possible to garner enough donations from individuals to raise the full budget.

However, even when medium and modest amounts of support could make a tremendous difference to a project, filmmakers often do not pursue this route of fundraising. The internal barriers are usually a fear of asking and a discomfort with being in a position of having to personally make an ask. It is so much easier to write a grant proposal than to sit across a table from someone, look them in the eye, and ask for support.

Fact is, there is no more effective way to get a donation than to make a person-to-person request; and, if money is needed quickly, there is no faster way to get support. Close this book right now, go make a phone call to a relative, and there might be a check in the mail tomorrow! If a filmmaker wants to get very good at fundraising, the internal impediments to making an "ask" must be addressed. Often the fear of rejection or the discomfort with requesting support can be overcome by remembering why the project is being made in the first place, and the importance it has for its potential audience. The filmmaker must feel, deep down, that the world will be a much better place once the film is completed.

One other upside to approaching individuals for support is that this type of fundraising has a healthy byproduct — it forces filmmakers to interact with the community, and brings the filmmaker face to face with a funder. When the check gets handed over, the donation becomes "personal" and the connection between the filmmaker and the funder is so much more real than when a grant is received through the mail. I recommend that the novice fundraiser conduct some role-playing exercises with friends to help practice asking scenarios and to begin to find some comfort level with dealing directly with donors.

THE PITCH

One of the very basic tools needed for all the fundraising avenues is the pitch — a very short statement that tells the listener what the film is about, who it is for, what is interesting or unusual about it, and that helps generate a conversation. How long should the pitch be? My recommendation is **no more than twenty seconds**! In other words, just long enough to pass the rigors of the infamous "elevator test":

If someone got on an elevator with me and asked what
I was working on, could I interest them in my project
before they reached the next floor?

If your pitch does not pass this test, it needs more work. Filmmakers often make the mistake of putting together lengthy descriptions of their projects and fail to remain sensitive to the fact that most people make up their minds about things very quickly. The listener has decided within a matter of seconds whether or not he is bored or intrigued by the filmmaker and the project being pitched. If the listener is bored, then talking for more than a minute is not going to help your cause. If the listener is intrigued, then the very best thing a filmmaker can do is to pause and allow questions so that a **dialogue** — and not a monologue — can take place.

Early in the project, create a short and exciting pitch that can be used in any and all settings. The pitch will get used thousands of times before the project is completed. There is no one perfect formula for creating a pitch because of the tremendous variety of projects and personalities. However, there are some guidelines that can help create a dynamic pitch. The screenwriter and author William Goldman (*Adventures in the Screen Trade*) gives some good advice about pitching:

- Be passionate
- Identify the audience
- Never forget whom you are talking to
- Be brief
- Remember you are not telling a story — you are throwing out a hook
- Keep it simple
- One or two lines
- Grab them
- Pitch ten times a day

In a *New York Times* interview (January 2, 2003), the producer Ismail Merchant (*Howard's End, Remains of the Day*) says the following about his talent for separating people from their money to finance a film: "It is, he said, a matter of 'injecting your enthusiasm about something you are doing, which you feel is so exceptional that it would be a pleasure for someone to be involved in it.'"

One of the most accomplished "pitchers" I know is independent filmmaker/producer Paul Devlin. Here are the pitches he used for three of his movies:

Super Star Dumb (*www.superstardumbmovie.com*)
Super Star Dumb *is a musical comedy about the broken promise of middle-class rock and roll stardom, following the story of a man punished by his talent in a society where anything short of celebrity is failure.*

Power Trip (*www.powertripthemovie.com*)
Power Trip *is about corruption, assassination, and street rioting over electricity in the former Soviet Republic of Georgia. It follows the story of an American company trying to solve the crisis there, but instead getting crushed by post-Soviet chaos.*

BLAST! (*www.blastthemovie.com*)
BLAST! *is about astrophysics Indiana Jones style! The story follows my brother, Mark Devlin, as he leads a tenacious team of scientists on the adventure of a lifetime from Arctic Sweden to the desolate ice of Antarctica to launch a revolutionary new telescope on a NASA high-altitude balloon to discover how the galaxies formed.*

BLAST! *is about the crazy lives of scientists. Their professional obsessions, personal and family sacrifices, and philosophical and religious questioning all give emotional resonance to a spectacular and suspenseful story of space exploration.*

PAUL DEVLIN'S PITCH ON PITCHING

Like many filmmakers, at first I had a hard time pitching my own projects. But I soon realized that I would forever be explaining what my movies were about, both in high-stress selling environments and casually to friends and acquaintances. So I decided I might as well get good at it. Here are some insights I've developed for successful pitching.

1. Distill your pitch
One or two sentences should be enough to get across the bare essence of any movie. Once you've done that you can layer and elaborate. But if

(continues)

PAUL DEVLIN'S PITCH ON PITCHING (cont.)

the first one or two sentences cannot stand alone, then you don't know your movie well enough yet. Developing the shortest pitch will help you understand your movie better. And that will help you communicate this more effectively to others, especially when you may have only a few short moments to capture someone's attention.

Notice that the pitch for *Super Star Dumb* is only one sentence — it leaves out narrative detail in favor of emphasis on theme, which resonates on its own, consistently generating empathy and discussion.

2. Layer your pitch

After you capture someone's attention, be prepared to develop and to embellish your pitch with more layers. The first sentence of the *Power Trip* pitch could stand alone if that's all that's required. But if there is opportunity, delivery of the second part builds more of the narrative elements.

Because of its science content, *BLAST!* has been mistakenly dismissed as marginal or "niche" by programmers. So the second part of that pitch corrects this preconception, emphasizing elements that demonstrate its appeal to a wider audience.

3. Start your pitch strong

Powerful and compelling words first. Draw them in right away.

After many false starts with words like "electricity," "Communism," and "Capitalism" for my *Power Trip* pitch, I found my best start was with these elements: "Corruption, assassination and street rioting..." No problem getting people's attention with those words.

Consider dropping words that may engender undesirable connotations. Notice *Super Star Dumb* uses "musical comedy" instead of "documentary." Expanding the conventional genre designation in this way is liberating and much more colorful.

I allow the word "scientist" in the pitch for *BLAST!* but the word "science" is deadly for programmers, so I make an effort to avoid it. "Space exploration" plays much better.

4. Memorize your pitch

No stumbling allowed! Memorizing your pitch gives you confidence always to discuss your movie assertively. Write out the pitch and then recite it over and over whenever you have the opportunity. If there are tough spots, consider a re-write to make it easier to memorize.

5. Feel your pitch

The pitfall of memorization is that, if you're not careful, it can make your pitch sound rote and hackneyed. Find ways to enliven your memorized pitch with enthusiasm so that you can inspire others. Acting classes help! (Recommended for filmmakers anyway.)   (*continues*)

PAUL DEVLIN'S PITCH ON PITCHING (cont.)

6. Slow down your pitch

Now that you've got your pitch distilled and memorized, there's plenty of time, no need to rush. Slow down. Now pause. Give your listener a moment to absorb what you just said. Now pitch them the rest. If you are asked to repeat it, then you know you've delivered it too fast.   (*continues*)

7. Evolve your pitch

As the movie and its distribution evolve, so does your pitch. You learn a lot about your movie as people respond to it. Steal copy from reviews and film festival blurbs and allow the best language to inform your pitch.

For example, the first line of my pitch for *BLAST!* — "astrophysics Indiana Jones style" — came straight from the description in the Sheffield Film Festival catalog.

8. Enjoy your pitch

Once you master the above, pitching becomes fun! Watching your listener's eyes widen in genuine interest at your movie is very gratifying. Ideally, you will inspire a lively discussion with your effective pitch.

Good luck, and good pitching!

A participant in one of my workshops told a story about the power a good pitch can have in almost any type of setting. The filmmaker was standing in line at a grocery store waiting to check out. The line was pretty long, and she ended up having a conversation with the man just behind her. At one point he asked her what she did for a living. She replied, "I'm a filmmaker." "Oh," he replied, "what an interesting profession. What are you working on now?" It was at this point that she used her pitch for a documentary she was doing that took place in Turkey. "My gosh," said the man, "I'm from Turkey! Tell me more about your project." The man asked for her business card before paying for his groceries. Three weeks later the filmmaker received a five-figure donation for her project. Never underestimate the power of a well-crafted pitch, and be ready to pitch *any-and-everywhere*.

QUALIFY THE DONOR

Once a list of possible donors has been identified (see my instructions for this in Chapter Two), the next important step is to "qualify" each of the donors — find out as much as possible about each person on the list. The kind of information needed includes:

- **Who the donor likes to support.** Individual donors are similar to private foundations in that they usually have a "theme" to their giving — a type of cause or area of interest where they want to give their support. This might be the arts and culture, animal rights, the environment, or any number of causes. It is very unusual for someone to be open to giving money to any and all types of nonprofit endeavors. Identify what they like.

- **What the donor likes to give.** Typically, individuals have the following types of things they like to donate: Money, Volunteer Time/Expertise, Professional Goods and Services. Some people like to write a check. Others are just more comfortable (either because of their economic standing or their philosophy) giving their time and expertise volunteering for a project. And still others like to give goods (equipment, for instance) or donated services (like catering). Once this information is known, the filmmaker can see if there is a good match for the needs of the project.

- **The donor's comfort level of giving.** Many a donation has been won or lost because of the amount requested. Individuals are funny about how they give money — they have a fairly narrow range of money that they typically give to their list of charities. For some people this might be $50 to $75 per ask. For others the range might be $5,000 to $6,000. This information must be researched and discovered *before* making an ask.

- **The approach that works best with the donor.** Although we know from statistics that the most effective approach to gaining a donation is an in-person meeting, it turns out that some donors are just highly resistant to this approach, or are more likely to give under a different scenario. For some donors, a written letter will be effective. For others, they will need to be asked by a peer, perhaps in a fundraising houseparty setting.

There are many ways to qualify the donor list. The very best way is to ask other people in the community who know the donor. One of the open secrets in donor relations is that there are very few secrets! The giving patterns of most people are fairly transparent and known by many other people. This is one reason I am fond of the fundraising brainstorming party where people help generate names of people and organizations who might give to a film project. Someone in that room is highly likely to be able to qualify the donor.

If it is hard to identify one person with knowledge of the donor's giving patterns, try working backwards. Find out what types of charities the donor likes, and what specific organizations the donor has supported. Check organization annual reports to see what amounts the donor typically gives to each (you will find the amounts are very similar). Contact one or two grantees personally and see if they will be willing to talk to you about the donor and provide some tips to help with the ask.

I met a filmmaker once in Los Angeles who told me how she got her first donation for her first documentary. She had been doing commercial work for corporate executives. When she started her personal project she remembered that one of the CEOs she knew had grown up in the neighborhood she planned to document. Before calling him up, she did a little research. She read the annual reports and program notes from local charities and discovered that he was a major donor to cultural causes, and liked to give $20,000 gifts. When she called, she pitched her project and asked permission to send the CEO a full project proposal. His reply was, "Of course I'd like to read your full proposal. I have a deep emotional connection to that neighborhood and I respect your work as a filmmaker. But first, why don't you just tell me how much you want to ask for." The filmmaker said, without hesitating, "What I could really use is $20,000 to help me do some more research, an initial shoot, and create a good fundraising clip." His reply was, "Don't bother to send me your proposal, I'm just going to go ahead and write you a check right now!" If the filmmaker had not "qualified" her donor, when she made the ask she might have made the tragic mistake of asking for $5,000 and then feeling lucky she had gained so much money, when in reality she would have lost $15,000.

Research is a basic task that must take place in every avenue of fundraising. Researching individual donors — their needs, desires, and giving patterns — is just as important as researching grants (covered later in this book). Now let's look at the various types of approaches.

ONE-ON-ONE

For many filmmakers — both novice and experienced — this is the most difficult type of ask to make. Even so, the in-person, face-to-face ask is the hardest one for a donor to resist. Try to make this type of ask happen whenever possible.

This approach will usually be easiest to arrange when the filmmaker — or someone close to the filmmaker — already knows the potential donor. The approach can begin with a phone call asking for a meeting. This might be followed up with a packet of information sent by mail or e-mail so that the donor has some time to look at and reflect on the project.

When the meeting does take place, it might be in an office, at a restaurant, at the donor's home, or at the filmmaker's loft or in an edit suite. When you can control the meeting place, try to keep it away from an office where your potential donor will have too many distractions. If the filmmaker is very shy and inexperienced at asking for money, then it would be smart to have a seasoned "buddy" along to help out. Find someone who is very comfortable asking for money, who is very knowledgeable about the project, and who will be respected by the donor. If the meeting is at a restaurant, the filmmaker must be prepared to pay for the meal. Scope out the restaurant before the appointment, and make sure seating will be at a table where there is a minimum of noise and other distractions. Before the meeting, be sure to have all your research ready about the donor, practice making the ask with a friend, and think about what would be the most appropriate way to dress.

The rhythm and science of making the ask is fairly simple:

◆ **Break the ice.** Take a few minutes just to have some introductory social conversation. Do not spend too much time socializing, however, because it is considered unprofessional. The donor is very aware of the purpose of the meeting and her time is precious.

◆ **Make your pitch.** Go ahead and pitch the project. Be brief and invite the donor to engage in a dialogue. Ideally, the donor will have many questions. Learn how to listen to the donor so you can pick up on likes and dislikes, and potential stumbling blocks to getting support.

- **Make a specific ask.** At some point it will be clear that the donor does not have any more questions, and that there is no more need to explain or describe the film. Now it is time to make a specific request for support. Here is what to do. Look the donor directly in the eyes (very important), ask for a specific amount of money, and say how it will be used. This approach might sound something like: "Well, if you don't have any more questions, then we both know why I am here today. I hope that you can make a donation of $7,500 to my project to help with the completion of the editing phase of the film."

- **Shut up.** There is a simple and powerful rule of thumb in the fundraising world: *After the ask, the first person to talk loses!* The best thing to do after the direct ask for support is simply to shut up, and to remain completely silent until the donor says something. Let the donor make the next move, no matter how long that silence may last. This can be a difficult moment for the filmmaker who, as the silence progresses, feels more and more uncomfortable and wants to interject with an apology. That would be a mistake. Sooner or later the donor is going to say something.

- **Respond.** After the donor says something it will be the film-maker's chance to respond. That response depends on which of three directions the donor has chosen to take:

1. *Acceptance.* If the donor says "Yes, I'll be happy to give you that donation," then be sure to say thanks and to find out: when and how to get the donation, what type of receipt the donor needs for tax purposes, and if the donor would like to receive recognition or would prefer to remain anonymous.

2. *Stall.* If the donor says "Maybe — let me have some more time to think about this," then find out if more information needs to be provided, and how much time the donor needs before being contacted again. Be sure to contact the donor again at the spec-ified time/date.

3. *Rejection.* If the donor says "I'm sorry, I'm not going to be able to help you out this year," then express your thanks for the time she took to hear the request, and politely ask if it is possible for her to tell you a bit more about why she could not support the project. A lot can be learned from a rejection if it is fully explained.

Every contact with a donor should be followed up with a thank-you note or an e-mail of some sort. Remember, fundraising is also community building — it is a way to help shore up your list of contacts that can make a difference to your career and to future films. Even a rejection from a donor can have an upside if the filmmaker has made a positive impression. As the project progresses, be sure to keep everyone contacted in the loop (including people who have said "no") through regular e-mails, newsletters, or press releases.

One of my clients keeps meticulous records of everyone who has ever given her a donation. She sends out a quarterly e-newsletter to keep everyone informed of her current project. Then, at the end of every year, she creates a "Year-end Wrap Up" that includes a form giving the opportunity to provide more support. She always gets a great response that includes donations from new people who received a copy of her note from a friend.

FUNDRAISING HOUSEPARTIES

I am not a fan of employing special events as ways to raise money for film projects — events where an admission fee is charged to a dinner, a benefit screening, an auction, or a concert. These types of events take a tremendous amount of energy and planning, involve large sets of people, often cost a great deal, and have the potential to end up losing money. My only exception to the rule of avoiding these is when the filmmaker: a) has a trusted set of volunteers in place who will take care of all the arrangements, and b) when all the costs are guaranteed and there is absolutely no chance of losing money (e.g., there is a corporate sponsor or all expenses are donated by the restaurant and entertainers).

What I do like is the fundraising houseparty. This is a wonderfully versatile form of fundraising appropriate for most projects. No one is charged admission to the party. People know when they are invited that if they come to the event they will be asked for support. These types of parties are great for generating support in the $3,000 to $7,000 range — although I have seen them garner much less when done in grassroots community settings, and much more when very wealthy individuals are involved. Another great advantage to this type of fundraising is that the filmmaker does not make the ask! That job is left to someone else who is a peer of those attending.

The first job is to find a supporter who is willing to donate his home or apartment to host an evening event, and who is also willing to invite friends and acquaintances. The filmmaker and host create an invitation that is sent out to a list of people three or four times larger than the number hoped for at the party. Because the invitation makes it clear that this is a fundraising event, many people will R.S.V.P. "no." But that is just fine, because those people who do decide to come have given their permission to be asked and are highly likely to give support.

The event itself should follow an agenda that will help maximize the likelihood of getting donations. Let people arrive and mingle for a while. Then sit everyone down for a formal presentation that includes: the host welcomes everyone; the filmmaker shows a short and, if possible, emotionally engaging sample from the film followed by a question and answer period; a peer who is well known and respected by the attendees stands up and makes a lucid and direct ask for money; people are allowed time to fill out a pledge card or write checks and use credit cards.

It is important after one of these parties to contact anyone who did not give support that night, but who did not say "No, I'm not interested in providing support at this time" on their pledge card. Follow-up calls to people who fit this "maybe" category will usually garner an additional 30% more in donations.

Below, Almudena Carracedo and Robert Bahar, producers of *Made in L.A.* (*www.madeinla.com*), share their thoughts and experiences raising funds for their documentary through houseparties. Successful events brought in an average of $8,000-10,000, although the filmmakers are quick to note that the amount raised will vary widely, depending on what is appropriate for a particular community or audience. Following several years of successful grassroots fundraising — including five of these houseparties — their film went on to receive support from ITVS, POV, and the Sundance Documentary Fund. *Made in L.A.* premiered in 2007 on the PBS POV series and went on to win a national Emmy Award.

TEN QUICK TIPS FOR
THROWING A GREAT HOUSEPARTY

1. **Identify the right core audience.** Everyone you invite should be deeply committed to your film being completed, either because they are passionate about your subject or because they want to support you as an artist. This is a symbiotic relationship: you need your core audience's support, and they need the film you are creating!

2. **Identify event "hosts" that will give you credibility** with your audience. These are the "early adopters" that will lend their names to your event and generate momentum; they may also contribute funds, spread the word, or volunteer to help.

3. **Set a realistic timeline and clear goals** for attendance, funds to be raised, and anything else you hope to achieve. You might also set "stretch" goals to encourage your team to go the extra mile!

4. **Reach out!** Your success will depend on your outreach and publicity. Luckily, you're not alone: your hosts can be of huge help by mobilizing their networks. Be innovative, contact press, use social networking tools like Facebook, MySpace, etc.

5. **Keep expenses down** so that funds end up "on the screen." Consider printing invitations yourself and asking local businesses for donations.

6. **Create multiple opportunities for donations.** Encourage hosts and sponsors to commit to "give or raise" a certain amount in advance. Include a remittance envelope in paper invitations and a "donate!" link in e-mails. Collect donations at the door, and do a pitch later in the event.

7. **Screen and discuss a five to ten-minute trailer** for your film. This gives the event an emotional focal point, makes your project real, and will inspire support!

8. **Let someone recognized in the community serve as a "cheerleader"** and make the final "ask" for you.

9. **Recognize the value of bringing together members of your core audience.** Listen to their compliments and criticisms, and consider their suggestions. Be sure to build an e-mail database — it will be very helpful down the road!

10. **Have fun!** The event should enjoyable, so don't forget music and good food. We love garden parties that give guests an opportunity to make new connections and catch up with old friends.

Almudena Carracedo and Robert Bahar
producers of *Made in L.A.*

For a very detailed explanation of this form of fundraising, along with sample invitations, refer to my book *The Fundraising Houseparty: How to Party with a Purpose and Raise Money for Your Cause – 2nd Edition.*[1]

LETTERS

There are whole categories of individuals who are easier to contact in writing than in person. The methods available to the filmmaker include letter-writing campaigns to a small group of donors, direct mail campaigns to large numbers of people, and e-mail letter appeals.

Whatever method chosen, there are a few rules that apply across the board to making any form of written approach to individual donors:

- **Keep the content emotion- and story-driven.** Try to capture the hearts of your readers and do not worry too much about facts or logic. This will not be true in other fundraising venues — with private foundations, for instance — but with individuals it is best to concentrate on involvement at an emotional level.
- **Personalize the appeal.** By "personalize" I mean see if there is a way to make the letter less generic by having it come directly from someone the donor already knows, or by having a friend of the donor at least place a short note at the bottom of the appeal letter. Personalizing the appeal will greatly increase the rate of donations, often by 50%.
- **Write a Postscript.** Studies of direct mail appeals show that readers often go to the end of the letter first! It is a smart idea to include a P.S. in every appeal letter, and be sure it makes an intriguing point and/or highlights a benefit. The job of the P.S. is to engage the reader, so that she goes to the lead and reads (or at least skims) the whole letter.
- **Make it easy to give.** Make it easy for the donor to respond and to make a donation. Tell the donor who to make the check out to, and enclose a self-addressed return envelope (with or without a stamp). If possible, let donors use a credit card, and allow

---

[1] Ordering information can be found on my Web site, *www.warshawski.com*

people the opportunity to volunteer to give you types of support other than money.

One of my clients received a donation from an individual for $4,000. The filmmaker asked the donor if he would be willing to write his friends and ask them for donations. The donor said "sure" but also indicated that he would not know what to say in the letter. The filmmaker offered to write the letter, which the donor then had reproduced on his own stationery. The donor sent the letter out to twelve friends, personally signed each with a short note at the bottom that said something like "Joe, I hope you can help out — this is a great project!" A few weeks later the filmmaker received three more donations of $4,000 each. Small letter-writing campaigns can be quite effective when they follow a peer-to-peer scenario.

Large direct mail campaigns are much harder to predict, and they can be a very risky endeavor. To make these campaigns work, the filmmaker needs a dynamite appeal letter — ideally written by a professional direct mail marketer — and an excellent mailing list. Because the letter will go to hundreds or even thousands of recipients, the costs (labels, photocopying, postage) can be quite high, so it is easy to lose money on this type of appeal. If direct mail looks like a route to take, then try to involve a professional, get photocopying donated if possible, and be sure to get mailing label lists that have a very high likelihood of being current and appropriate for the project. One way around the cost of distribution is for the filmmaker to find a newsletter or magazine that likes the project so much they are willing to include a one-page appeal in one of their mailings.

THE WORLD WIDE WEB AND ITS MANY TENTACLES

Another burgeoning avenue for fundraising campaigns has opened itself to the filmmaker: The Internet. The Internet provides a powerful way to access individual donors. The Internet is a visual medium and offers many opportunities to display clips or scenes from current and previous films. E-mail reaches people instantaneously, and there is no postage cost for delivery! It costs just as much to reach thousands of people as it does to reach just one person. The great roadblock to e-mail fundraising is that the filmmaker has to avoid the appearance of sending "spam" — junk e-mail. There is much more ill will and anger generated by spam e-mail than by paper junk mail sent through the post office. Here are some general rules that will help make an e-mail campaign successful:

- **Create a Web site and/or a Blog.** An e-mail appeal almost always will direct the reader to a Web site where much more information can be found on the film and the filmmaker, and where there is a form that makes it easy to make a donation and/or to ask for more information. More and more filmmakers have their own Web sites and blogs, and smart filmmakers are beginning to take advantage of the Internet's capabilities for fundraising, as well as for marketing and promotion.

- **Get connected.** The best way for an e-mail appeal to be accepted by the reader is if the letter is coming from a trusted source. Find organizations that might have a vested interest in seeing the film succeed, and ask that they allow an announcement to go out to members on their e-mail list, and/or that mention of the film with a hyperlink placed on their own Web site.

- **Get permission.** When using e-mail to approach new people, send each e-mail out to one person at a time, use their name and ask their permission to write back with information about your project. Promise that your note is a "one time only" mailing and that no further communication will take place unless the respondent gives permission to be contacted.

- **Be specific.** Desperate cries for general support are likely to be ineffective. Come up with specific amounts for specific parts of the project. Keep the copy short and engaging, and please check for spelling and grammar errors.

- **Be smart.** In your day-to-day correspondence, be sure to add a short tag line at the end of every e-mail you send out that says something about the new film, where people can go for more information about it (a URL hyperlink), and how they can give support.

The Web has had a dramatic effect on how filmmakers are doing individual fundraising. The key to getting individual donations is to identify a constituency — your "community" — and then connect with them. In the past this was difficult to do. Now with the social networking capabilities of the Internet there are many more avenues for finding and involving individuals who might be interested in your film. As an example, look at this portion of an e-blast I received from filmmaker Jenny Deller about her feature film *Future Weather.*

Dear Friends:

I arrived in New York for IFP's Independent Film Week the day before Lehman Brothers declared bankruptcy. The conference had gotten off to a fairly uninspired start with the first panel repeating the tired line that film financing begins with finding a star. Now, thirty blocks south, Wall Street was seizing up in what promised to be a prolonged panic. This, I thought, does not bode well for *Future Weather,* my little indie that could.

But as my eyes adjusted to the brightness of such indie film luminaries as the Director of Sundance Film Fest, the CEO of Rainbow Media (parent to IFC and the Sundance Channel), and the president of Sony Pictures Classics, I realized there was no reason to lose heart.

Jittery times in the indie film world have been going on for several years now. Studios are shuttering their specialty divisions; Sundance is no longer the site of midnight bidding wars; foreign pre-sales are down; and with the advent of cheap HD cameras, independent film production is at an all-time high, meaning a much, much, *much* more crowded playing field.

But this changing climate has just forced filmmakers to be *more* creative and *more* independent in their fundraising, marketing, and distribution strategies — grassroots adjustments that are ultimately giving them more control over their product and their revenues.

We heard about digital distribution from the producer/directors of *The Cult of Sincerity,* web series *The West Side,* and design doc *Helvetica;* self-distribution from the producers of Sundance favorite *Good Dick* and the social change doc *Made in L.A.*; and crowd-sourcing from the pioneer of distribution experiments, Lance Weiler, director of *Head Trauma* and creator of the open-source *Workbook Project.* Not a star in any of them.

They were incredibly inspiring stories of successful projects, and the thing they all had in common was you: the fan. From donating and organizing to simply spreading the word, audience members are interacting with films at an unprecedented level. And it's working to get films made and seen. The key, we were told, was growing our fan base before production even begins.

So one of our goals this fall at Future Weather Productions is to triple the number of people we touch. You can help us. It means trusting that your actions — however tiny — actually matter and taking not just one, but *multiple* actions. Pick at least two:

* Forward this letter to friends you think would be interested in *Future Weather* and ask them to check out *our Web site*
* Our *mailing list subscription box* is in the lower right-hand corner of the page (hint, hint)
* Join our Facebook Cause
* And after you do, tell a friend (or ten) about it
* Leave a comment on our *blog*
* Better yet, add a link to it on yours
* Better still, pitch us a story related to the environment or green filmmaking and get published!
* Become our friend on the social network where you hang out: MySpace... Twitter... Facebook...
* Do the *YouTube* thing! our trailers are there and viewable, sharable and embeddable
* Send us your ideas! Let's interact!

Every minute of support you've given us over the last six months has increased our momentum. We are going to make *Future Weather,* and we can't do it without you.

Jenny

www.futureweathermovie.com

Note how Jenny ends her e-mail with very direct options for involvement, many of them utilizing social network sites.

Director Robert Greenwald and producer Jim Gilliam of Brave New Films (*Wal-Mart: The High Cost of Low Price*) are masters at getting donations from individuals over the Internet. It's a movement they call "People-Powered Film." To quote a profile from the *Washington Post*: "You have an idea. You have an affinity group. You have e-mail addresses. You ask for money." When they began working on their documentary *Iraq for Sale: The War Profiteers*, Greenwald and Gilliam knew they would have trouble fundraising through traditional channels. Of the $750,000 needed, they could count on about $450,000 from DVD sales, foreign rights, and retail store advances. That left $300,000 to raise. They found a donor who offered $100,000, but only if they could match it with the remaining $200,000. The filmmakers sent out a mass email appeal to everyone in their database who had ever bought a DVD or had made contact with them. They received $267,892 in just 10 days ($185,000 from 3,000 donors averaging $62 each, and a major donor at $82,000).

IndieGoGo.com is an online social marketplace that "connects filmmakers and fans to make independent film happen." They have learned a lot about what it takes to fundraise effectively on the Web. Here are some things they recommend based on their work with independent filmmakers:

IndieGoGo 101
ELEVEN STEPS TO KICKSTART
YOUR FUNDRAISING ONLINE

• **Production Is the New Promotion** — It's never too early to get started. Build your fan base and funding Obama style, "early and often."

• **Create an Online Presence** — Create a Web site, embrace social networks (Facebook, MySpace, IndieGoGo), and take advantage of social media (YouTube, Google) to get your message out.

• **Capture the E-mail Address** — There is nothing more valuable than creating a relationship with your audience and staying in touch. It all starts with capturing the e-mail address. Capture it online, via mobile, or simply use sign-up sheets. *(continues)*

IndieGoGo 101 (cont.)

• **Use Widgets** — Like bumper stickers for the Internet, widgets let you and your fan base spread your message far and wide using a little "copy, paste."

• **Create a Pitch Clip** — Make it personal, concise, and heartfelt. Three minutes is a good length, but best to err on the short side and end with a clear call to action. You can't be everywhere, so let technology be everywhere for you.

• **Identify the Audience** — It is important to know who will want your film. Every topic has a following. The next step is to size and target the potential audience.

• **Identify Assets / VIP Perks** — Credits in the film, pre-sold DVDs, invitation to the cast party, or even an authentic piece of Saddam Hussein's rug — every project has exclusive perks that can be offered to the audience. This way the customer feels more connected.

• **Work with Influencers** (bloggers, organizations, and brands) — It's important for DIWO (Do-It-With-Others) filmmakers to find amazing partners. Every film covers topics that certain bloggers and organizations care about. Every blogger and organization also needs to provide their readers and members with interesting content and opportunities. Let your film be the cool perk they offer. Work with partners to spread your message to their audience. Brands — like organizations — are eager to partner with films to offer relevant content to their customers. It's a win-win.

• **Raise a Dialogue** — Too often the Internet is used only to broadcast a message. Instead, use all the tools available (blogs, RSS, Twitter, user generated content, etc.) to create a *two-way communication*. Engage the audience with questions and they will respond.

• **Go Offline** — Online is great, but nothing is better than starting a relationship by meeting someone face to face. Make sure to attend conferences, festivals, houseparties and industry events. Share your card or website. Independent of meeting place, the next step is to lead them to the Internet (i.e. IndieGoGo profile) to take action.

• **It's a Marathon, Not a Sprint** — Keep your content fresh. Consistently update your fans so you can build a trusting, loyal fan base over time. Every action will lead you to your next fan and next success.

Slava Rubin, Founder

We'll be hearing more about the Web later in the book in the section on "Alternative Strategies" for fundraising.

Before we leave this chapter I want to mention one other advantage to pursuing individual donations: morale. I said earlier that individual donations usually arrive in small and modest amounts, and that they tend to trickle in intermittently, especially if any type of letter-writing campaign is taking place. The upside is that this trickle is great for lifting the spirits of the filmmaker and her team. Donations arrive in the mail at unexpected moments and are a great boost to morale, especially during periods when it is proving difficult to get support from foundations or corporations. But the main advantages to pursuing individuals will always be that they are the fastest way to get support, they provide the largest pool of possible support, and they keep the filmmaker very connected to the community.

CHAPTER FIVE

THE PAPER TRAIL: Foundations and Government Agencies

> "Assuming your cause is just, planning is needed to achieve success.... Do what is right and you will be rewarded. Move forward and you will get support.... As you succeed, continue with self-discipline and self-restraint.... You will be accepted and entrusted with leadership. You will have good fortune without seeking it.... There is no obstacle in your path."
> —I Ching: The Book of Changes *(translated by Frank J. MacHovec)*

Private foundations and government agencies (I'll just say "foundations" for the rest of this chapter) require a completely different approach from that employed with individual donors. The major difference lies in the fact that organizational funders require a good deal of paperwork. Almost all will want to see a formal written proposal that goes before a panel of trustees before any money is awarded.

Grants have traditionally been an important source of support for noncommercial film projects. Even as the fortunes of these sources wax and wane with the vagaries of the economy and of politics, filmmakers will want to keep this type of support in the mix of income streams when and where appropriate. The great thing about grant support is that it typically comes in good-sized chunks (in the thousands of dollars) and that this support proves a great boon to giving the filmmaker credibility and enticing other support. Filmmakers must keep in mind, however, that attracting foundation support can be a lengthy process, and that this avenue of fundraising should be part of a long-range plan.

RESEARCH

In Chapter Two I list the basic ways to do research on foundations and government agencies. Just like the instructions on qualifying the donor for individual donations, the rule of "research first" is true for agencies. It should be very clear by now that the principle of doing good basic and thorough research is primary to any and every type of fundraising for film.

The filmmaker's goal during research is to whittle the potential list of foundations down to the most probable candidates, and to discover as much of the following information as possible:

◆ What is the foundation's mission? What is its particular focus for funding this year?
◆ What are the deadlines for application?
◆ What information does the foundation expect in a full grant proposal?
◆ Who, and for what types of projects, has the foundation provided funding recently?
◆ What size of grants does the foundation like to make?
◆ What criteria are used for judging proposals?
◆ What is the name, phone number, and e-mail address of the program officer that will oversee the filmmaker's proposal?

Before hitting the books, the filmmaker has to begin thinking like a foundation program officer. This starts by understanding that very, very few foundations are interested in funding film as an art form. In 2006, here is how foundations divvied up their funds (as reported by The Foundation Center):

- Education – 23%
- Health – 23%
- Human Services – 14%
- **Arts & Culture – 12%**
- Public/Society Benefit – 11%
- Environment & Animals – 6%
- International Affairs – 5%
- Science & Technology – 3%
- Religion – 2%
- Social Science – 1%

Within the category "Arts & Culture" there are only a handful of places (8%) that fund films primarily because of a devotion to film and filmmakers. The vast majority of funders fund a film primarily because it is an excellent way to get a message across about their particular area of interest that year — the environment, health, education, etc. These funders are primarily interested in how a film can benefit the public.

It is a major mistake to find the texts on foundations, jump to the subject index and look only under "film, video, media, television." Remember, many foundations are funding the film not *because* it is a film, but *in spite of* the fact that it is a film! So, spend the vast majority of research time looking under the appropriate subject categories for the film being made — that's where the money is hiding.

First create a long laundry list of possibilities. Next, do a deeper layer of research on each of these possibilities. Request annual reports and copies of formal guidelines, and visit their Web sites. It is not uncommon to discover that some of the foundations on the list have geographic limitations that exclude the project, or that their subject interest this year does not perfectly match the focus of the film. This process will help whittle the first long list down to something much more manageable.

Call up people and organizations that have received grants from each foundation (they will be listed in the annual reports) and ask about their experiences with the foundation, what recommendations they have for improving your chances for success, and who is the appropriate person to contact. This is the very best way to finish up your research. People who have dealt recently with the foundation have the most current and accurate information possible.

Do not be dissuaded initially by foundation guidelines that say "we don't fund media." If the project feels like a very strong match for the foundation's target area of interest, then do not give up hope yet. Many films have been funded by foundations that said "we don't fund media" when they were approached in the right way by a convincing filmmaker with a very strong project and proposal.

YOUR APPROACH: IT'S PERSONAL

Here is part of a letter written to me by Ralph Arlyck, independent filmmaker (*Godzilla Meets Mona Lisa, Following Sean*).

> "Phone vs. writing: I imagine you advocate as much personal contact as possible — face-to-face if feasible, phone over letters, and so on. I know the conventional wisdom about the importance of talking to people, that one has to demonstrate one's passion for the subject, the project, etc., but one also has to understand one's own strengths. I can be adequate on the phone, but I'm not irresistible. I'm better in person and I'm best of all writing. (Unfortunate progression, but there it is.) So my general approach tends to be to send people the press kit and a cover letter which says that I'll be calling them in a week or so. I would say the most common response when I do call is that the material never arrived, never got to the targeted person, they've forgotten, etc. Usually I speak not to the person in question but to an assistant who says, if he/she remembers the project, that they have my application and will be getting back to me by mail. A few weeks later the rejection letter comes. I'm courteous and friendly with the administrative assistants and frequently have nice conversations with them but the eventual answer is almost always the same."

Ralph is typical of most filmmakers: he would love to be able to raise lots of money by submitting written proposals and avoiding making personal contact with funders. Filmmakers can, indeed, get some grants primarily or solely on the basis of a written document. However, *70% of all grants awarded in the U.S. have involved some form of personal contact!* Filmmakers who do not attempt to make personal contact with the funder are bucking the odds and not being as effective as possible. There is a favorite saying among fundraisers that goes: "People give to people." **The more the filmmaker attempts and is successful at personally engaging the funder, the higher the likelihood of success in obtaining grant support.**

Why is this true? For one thing, as I noted in the chapter on individual fundraising, it is just harder to say "no" to someone with whom the funder has made a connection. More important with foundations is the elusive factor of "trust." What is it that makes a foundation feel comfortable with entrusting tens of thousands of dollars to an individual filmmaker? A good written proposal, of course, helps. But funders are smart enough to know that anyone can hire a good grantwriter to grind out a proposal. The tipping point is created by the filmmaker himself. Has he made the kind of impression on the funder that convinces them that they can trust him to complete and distribute a great product? As the head of a small family foundation once said to me: "What I look for when I meet the filmmaker is that quality that makes me feel the filmmaker will walk through fire, climb mountains, and swim across oceans if need be to finish and distribute a film."

This is why, the next step after research is to call the foundation directly and speak with the appropriate program officer. Many foundations in their guidelines will suggest as the initial contact that you "send a letter of inquiry prior to submitting a formal proposal." Whenever possible, do not make this the first form of contact — especially with foundations that say "we don't fund media" in their guidelines. It is far too easy for foundations to *pro forma* toss aside good project ideas by just sending back a standard rejection form letter that may have been signed by a secretary or receptionist on the basis of a simple instruction from the CEO that says "Don't show me any applications that have the words *film, video, media, radio,* or *television* in them."

When I conduct workshops on fundraising I encourage an informal process called "testify," which allows anyone to stand up and spontaneously testify about something they just heard that has a lot of resonance to them. During one workshop when I talked about the letter of inquiry, a young woman stood up and told the following story. A year earlier she had been working on a documentary project about a degenerative disease. One day she opened up the newspaper and noticed that the CEO of a local corporate foundation had a child with this particular disease. The filmmaker was sure that the CEO would want to support her project, so she crafted a strong letter of inquiry to his foundation even though the guidelines said, "We don't fund media." The next week she received a standard rejection form letter from the foundation. Naturally, she was disappointed. A month later, she found herself at a fancy reception and by chance ran into the CEO. During their conversation, he asked the filmmaker what projects she was working on. When she mentioned her documentary, his interest was immediately piqued. He said, "You should definitely send a proposal to my foundation. We don't normally fund media projects, but I'm sure we would seriously consider giving you some support." She replied, "I'm embarrassed to tell you this, but I already sent in a letter of inquiry and received a rejection note." The CEO looked her in the eye and told her he had never seen that letter of inquiry, and that she should forward a full proposal directly to his attention. Soon thereafter she received a substantial grant from the very same foundation that had previously rejected her on the basis of a letter of inquiry.

There will be times when sending a brief letter of inquiry cannot be avoided — when there is no phone or e-mail contact information for the foundation, or when the program officer just refuses to chat with you without getting paperwork first. But many foundations will have at least a short conversation with you first, if you are courteous, brief, and ask intelligent questions.

The goal of the filmmaker at this stage is to find ways to make the funder understand and like the project so much, and have such great respect for and trust in the filmmaker, that the program officer does everything in her power to help make sure the filmmaker gets support from her foundation.

Begin by calling the foundation and asking to speak with the appropriate program officer. Hopefully, the filmmaker already has the name of the right person to contact. If not, then the art of "getting past the secretary" will have to be mastered. My advice here is simple: make the secretary love you, don't be obnoxious, and never leave more than one message, if any.

Another way to get past the secretary quickly is to name-drop. If it is possible to get referred to the foundation by someone already known to them, then dropping that person's name will often get the caller through to the program officer very quickly. Be warned, however, that this tactic can only be used when the person whose name is being mentioned has given permission for the use of her name. Here is what filmmaker Julia Reichert (*A Lion in the House*) wrote me recently: "What also seems to work like a charm is to have a name to drop. For XYZ Foundation, I called a grantee at Harvard (go to the top!) and chatted with her about her work and my work, and she was fine with my using her name in calling XYZ. I had tried previously with no success to get someone on the phone. But by using her name, I got a call back right away."

Once the appropriate program officer is reached, begin any and all conversations with a foundation by saying something that shows understanding of its current mission and area of focus. Here is a typical call scenario:

> *"Hello, my name is Morrie Warshawski. I under-stand your foundation is interested this year in issues of sustainability and saving the tropical rain forests of Brazil."*
>
> *"Yes, that's true. But I'm very busy, all our informa-tion is in our printed guidelines, and we prefer to receive a letter of inquiry prior to any other contacts."*
>
> *"Yes, I understand that. I have read all your infor-mation thoroughly, and I'm prepared to send you a letter of inquiry. However, I have just a couple of quick ques-tions I wanted to ask first because they are not covered in any of your written materials."*
>
> *"Well, in that case, you can have two minutes. What do you want to ask?"*

Now the filmmaker must quickly and effectively pitch the project, follow up with an intelligent question, and hope to engage the funder in an interesting conversation. The funder may say, "Don't waste your time — that project has no chance with us." Or, as is often the case, the funder might say, "That sounds interesting. Tell me a little more." If the scenario goes well, the funder will invite you to submit a full proposal, and will even offer some specific suggestions for how to improve your chances for success.

Let's hear what a funder — Jon Jensen of the George Gund Foundation — had to say about this phone call (taken from an interview in Andy Robinson's excellent book *Grassroots Grants: An Activist's Guide to Proposal Writing*):

> *Call foundation staff and tell them what you're doing. Give them a quick, simple description of your project — no more than 90 seconds — then ask your questions. I can think of a number of proposals I would have declined to support without first having had a phone conversation and forming a positive opinion about the person on the other end of the line... If you get me on the phone you get five times as much information as we list in our guidelines. This is by design: we want to be responsive, not prescriptive. My job is to demystify the process — I tell you everything I can at every stage of the game. I can also help you identify the strengths and weaknesses of your proposal and the obstacles you'll need to overcome if you want to get funded... Foundation-wise applicants know how to time the asking of the key question: "What are our chances of getting a grant?" It is often an unasked question because the applicant doesn't want to hear the answer. If asked at the appropriate time, however, this question can save the grant seeker a great deal of time, labor, and anxiety.*

It is instructive to keep in mind the types of things that foundations worry about, and the criteria they apply to judging a media proposal. Here is a sample list of evaluation criteria from a funder of social issue media, Diana Barrett of The Fledgling Fund:

FROM THE DESK OF DIANA BARRETT, President, The Fledgling Fund (www.thefledglingfund.org)

Setting the Stage

In our current application cycle we received close to 200 letters of inquiry in our Creative Media area, which focuses the use of media to advance social change. We invited 82 to submit proposals. Most of these projects are films in various stages of completion but there were a number that focused on leveraging Web 2.0 technologies. As a funder of social change media, our emphasis is increasingly on outreach: on engaging communities through increased awareness of the issue and of possible solutions. The film is important, but we view it as a launching pad for a larger campaign with clear goals and, when possible, a call to action.

As we assess the proposals and make difficult choices about which ones to fund, we use a set of "screens" or questions that we apply to all projects in a an effort to make the process fair to applicants and useful to our small staff. At present, these are as follows:

#1. Quality. This may seem obvious, but we receive many great advocacy pieces that on paper are timely and important, but we want to be sure that the film or other media tells the story with a compelling narrative, strong characters that we care about, a clear story arc. We ask whether the project tells a universal story and whether it tells it well.

#2 Potential for Social Impact. Another critical factor is the social impact of the project: Does it add to or advance our understanding of the issue? Is it a unique perspective? Is this project likely to make a difference? Is it likely to change attitudes and perhaps behavior? Certain films accomplish this task even in the course of production, engaging audiences through a Web site and community-based activities. Some change attitudes later. This is often difficult to assess but something that is a key focus for us.

#3 Strength of the Outreach Proposal. Filmmakers seldom have a thorough outreach plan, particularly if they are still in postproduction, and we understand that. But we do look for an understanding of target audiences, constituencies that would be interested in the topic, and in some cases relationships with specific NGOs that already work on the issue and would be interested in using the film as a vehicle for change.

#4 Does the project move the field forward? We sometimes really love a film and then find that the story it's telling is one-sided and partisan and in some cases misleading. Other times, it may be commonly held wisdom by one or more constituents but not be a message that we want to disseminate widely, particularly if the other viewpoint is not presented. We look for projects that can move the dialogue and debate forward in a productive way.

(continues)

FROM THE DESK OF DIANA BARRETT (cont.)

#5 Does the project have strong leadership? We look for a filmmaker who is committed to the issue, one who really cares. While he or she may be chafing to make the next film, he's willing to stay with this one, use our help to devise a really innovative outreach plan, be willing to travel with the film and take the necessary time to use the film in a broad variety of ways. This often means that the filmmaker has to be flexible and willing to repurpose the film for different audiences.

#6 Can the project be completed with Fledging Funding? We are a small foundation, and have to make sure that the project will be finished. If we're part of a funding group, we're delighted to play a participatory role but we need to assure ourselves that either our funds alone, or commingled with other monies, will indeed bring the film to completion so that it can achieve its overall goals.

Before moving on to writing the proposal, let's hear what one more funder had to say about what things the foundation thinks about when scanning a filmmaker's proposal (taken from an interview with the Playboy Foundation in the December 2000 issue of *The Independent*):

> *First I look at the paperwork: Will the subject matter advance or promote the Foundation's mission? What is the filmmaker's experience in making films and raising money? Who are the other funders? Can the filmmaker raise enough money or find enough backers to see the project through to completion? What is the distribution plan? Who is its intended audience? Is there a fiscal sponsor? etc. Then I sit down and look at the trailer or rough cut: How does it look? Does it do what the filmmaker intended? Will the Foundation be proud to have its name associated with the project? If the answers are in the affirmative to most of these questions, we usually award it a grant. I only compare one film to another when a project has been done before. Then I ask myself, what makes this one different or better?*

WRITING THE PROPOSAL

Now, finally, the grant can be written. There are stacks of books available on the art of grantwriting. What I hope the reader has understood by now is that the written proposal is just the tip of the iceberg. If the filmmaker has followed all of my instructions up until now, then the act of creating the grant should be a simple matter of pulling together many elements that are already in place, and creating just a few more items we have not yet discussed. The filmmaker with strong writing skills can create the entire document himself, and then call on a colleague to give it a once-over. The filmmaker with poor-to-average writing skills will have to work with a partner, or hire a professional grantwriter for assistance.

There are a few general rules that apply to almost any type of grantwriting. First, be sure to find out exactly what the funder wants to see. Most funders have specific guidelines that ask for information of a certain type, and usually of a certain length. *Always follow the guidelines of the funder!* If the filmmaker wants to alter the guidelines by adding more information, or additional types of support materials, then the rule is to ask permission from the funder first. In fact, this type of question is an excellent excuse to call the funder and deepen your relationship. Otherwise, only send what is requested in the format and length the funder has enumerated.

Next, keep some stylistic rules in mind. Make the prose of the grant as simple and direct as possible. Stay away from very long convoluted sentences with many dependent clauses. Use plain English, and employ as many bullets or subheads as necessary to help organize the proposal. Make it easy for funders to find any bit of information they want at a moment's notice; or, as the saying goes, "Can't scan it? Can it!"

Another important principle is to strike a balance between mind and heart, reason and passion. When writing letters to individual donors I counsel erring toward the side of passion — to make the letters as heartfelt and emotional as possible. That would be a mistake with foundations. In this arena the proposal must convince the funder that the filmmaker is both passionately committed to the project and a credible and levelheaded person who can be trusted to create a quality program. Show too much passion and lose the funder's respect. Show too much intellect without any passion, and the funder begins to wonder about your power to stay the course when the going gets tough.

With respect to producing the document, never put your information on fancy colored or textured paper, and never use expensive bindings or covers — funders frown on this since it is considered a waste of money. Keep in mind that the funder may have to take the proposal apart as soon as it is received and make multiple copies for the Board of Trustees. Use plain white paper (8 ½" × 11" only — never any larger) and a plain font 12-point typeface (Times Roman, Book Antiqua, Garamond, Arial, and Courier are quite common). Smaller type may get more information on each page, but that makes the writing much harder to read — especially for any funder who is farsighted. I actually heard a trustee say once that he rejected a grant because it was just too hard to read the words on the page. Some funders will allow transmission of a proposal by e-mail as a file attachment, and/or on a disk; if that's the case, be sure the software formats for text and attachments are compatible.

The Independent Television Service (ITVS) has become one of the major funders of independent films. Here is what Claire Aguilar, Vice President of Programming, has to say about submitting a successful application to them. (In the Appendix you will find a sample of an ITVS proposal that actually received funding.)

SEVEN TIPS FOR PRODUCERS WHEN APPLYING FOR FUNDING FROM ITVS

1. **Read the Guidelines and Application Instructions Thoroughly and Follow Them.** This tip sounds so simple and one should assume that it goes without saying — but like any instruction manual, it is essential to go over the guidelines very carefully and to follow them before filling out the application. Some pitfalls to avoid:

   - **Submit the proposal online, and ALSO submit the paper and required (video) materials** — some applicants do not submit their hard copy proposals and video materials and then they are disqualified.

   - **Deadlines are not flexible** — we need to receive them in the office by the deadline date or they will not be accepted. *(continues)*

SEVEN TIPS FOR PRODUCERS (cont.)

- **Read the fine print on the guidelines and application.** The ITVS award is not a grant, it is a contract agreement, thus certain requirements and deliverables must be accepted (because of FCC guidelines, your project must adhere to broadcast standards).

- **Do not submit extra materials** — letters of recommendation, graphics or illustrations, gifts or personal director statements are not required — the materials will be reviewed by staff and evaluators based on the required materials only.

- **Use 10-point font or larger** — don't try to cram everything in your treatment pages because of limited space. The evaluators appreciate clear and clear writing — and size 10 font or larger is easier on the eyes.

2. **Budget your project realistically.** If you under-budget your project, that does not mean that you have a greater chance of being approved. If you over-budget your project, this will be taken into account and can jeopardize the approval. Each initiative has different budget thresholds and is indicated in the guidelines. For example, Open Call does not require an itemized budget in the first phase, but does require that you indicate the request amount and what money has been already raised. The average request for Open Call is between $80,000 and $250,000 for a one-hour documentary.

3. **Tell your story in the treatment.** Write a treatment, not a treatise — tell a story, not history. Don't list events or dwell on past events or context and history. Your treatment should include your vision and style as a producer or director, as well as information and context to understand the story. Incorporate your passion into the treatment, but don't resort to superlatives and empty market-speak to describe your project. Have someone else read your proposal before submitting — if a colleague can't understand your story, ITVS evaluators won't either. For useful information about how to write a treatment, see the ITVS essay "Writing a Better ITVS Treatment" at *http://itvs.org/ producers/treatment.html.*

4. **Consider the ITVS mission and what the program will bring to public television — look at the criteria and state in your application how they would apply to your film so that it would be an appropriate fit for ITVS.** For example, discuss how the film would target an under-represented audience (minority communities, seniors, youth, physically and mentally challenged), or how your film would be appropriate for those communities. Talk about your relationship with underrepresented communities — whether through access, personal or professional

(continues)

SEVEN TIPS FOR PRODUCERS (cont.)

experience or research. Discuss how the story is untold and deserves attention, or what fresh perspectives you would give to a story that already seems to have been told.

5. **For the funding initiatives, remember that the process takes four to six months for a final response.** Think about this timeline for your project — if you are in production and will finish before the final recommendation in five months' time, then it wouldn't be appropriate to apply to Open Call. Urgent cases — where timely events or subjects that are old or dying must be recorded immediately, do not hasten funding or make a more compelling argument for greenlighting.

6. **Include samples that exemplify your best work, whether it is a past completed sample or a demo of your work in progress.** Remember that evaluators will watch up to ten minutes of your current demo, so clearly indicate what you would like to present, whether it is a trailer, work-in-progress, scene selects or footage.

7. **Be open to ITVS feedback — every applicant to ITVS is given feedback by staff if requested.** Even if your application doesn't make it, you can reapply, and hopefully use the feedback from staff and evaluators to improve your proposal the next time you apply.

ELEMENTS OF A FULL GRANT PROPOSAL

Because every proposal is going to be different, and tailored specifically for each funder, there is no one standard format that will suffice. However, I like to have my clients pull together in advance everything they might ever need so that they are ready for any and every proposal scenario.

Here is an outline of what I consider a full grant proposal:

1. COVER LETTER
2. TITLE PAGE
3. TABLE OF CONTENTS
4. FORMAL REQUEST
5. DESCRIPTION OF THE PROJECT
6. STATEMENT PROVING NEED
7. DESCRIPTION OF INTENDED AUDIENCE
8. WHY I BECAME INVOLVED WITH THIS PROJECT
9. TREATMENT
10. PRODUCTION PLANS & TIMELINE

11. PERSONNEL
12. DISTRIBUTION PLANS
13. COMMUNITY OUTREACH
14. EVALUATION PLAN
15. FUNDING STRATEGY FOR COMPLETION OF
    PROJECT
16. BUDGETS
17. MISCELLANEOUS SUPPORT MATERIALS
    a. FISCAL SPONSOR LETTER
    b. LETTERS OF SUPPORT
    c. LETTERS OF COMMITMENT
    d. PRESS CLIPPINGS
    e. FULL RÉSUMÉS OF PERSONNEL
    f. DEMO REEL/TRAILER

Let's take a look at each of these elements to gain a bit more clarity on what the filmmaker needs to produce to make each section credible.

- **Cover Letter.** Very simply, the filmmaker writes a one-page introductory note on letterhead, and reminds the funder of their previous conversations. The filmmaker will want to say here how much money is being requested and what the funds will be used for. Thank the funder for accepting the proposal for consideration. Offer to be available to answer any questions that might come up. Be sure to say, "I will be calling in a few days just to make sure this package arrived safely and to see if you might have any questions you'd like to ask me before the proposal goes to panel." If other funders have already given to the project, be sure to mention that in this cover note. And, include a P.S. that reiterates some important point.

- **Title Page.** Keep it simple. Don't forget to include all necessary contact information including name, address, phone, fax, e-mail and Web address. It is good to place under the title of the film, its intended length and format and, possibly, the major audience for whom the film is intended. If an image has been chosen to represent the film, it can be placed here as well.

- **Table of Contents.** This is necessary only if the proposal is fairly lengthy, for it helps funders find sections easily.

◆ **Formal Request.** This is your introductory paragraph that quickly describes the project, the portion of the project for which you want support (e.g., script development and writing, editing, community outreach, etc.), and the exact amount of money you want. *Be sure that the amount of the request has been cleared with the funder before writing the proposal.* This will be the last call made to the program officer before writing the grant. The filmmaker should, through research, already have discovered what the funder's comfort zone of giving is. But things change, and the only way to know if the funder still gives out a certain size grant is to ask directly. I would call my contact at the foundation just before submitting the proposal and say: "I'm glad you have agreed to allow me to send in a full proposal and I'm almost ready to finish my document. I'm calling just to make sure that the foundation will be comfortable with my request for $13,000." If you have a good relationship with the program officer, then you will probably get an honest answer that either confirms that this amount is still doable, or that suggests a lower or even higher request. Many a grant request to a foundation has been won or lost just on the basis of the amount of the request.

◆ **Description of the Project.** Here the filmmaker can spend more time explaining what the project is about, the approach that will be taken, what topics will be covered and in what depth, and the intended outcome.

◆ **Statement Proving Need.** This is where the filmmaker takes as much time and space as necessary to prove that the world needs this program. This is a good place to mention a few other programs that have already been made about the same topic, or in the same genre, and to differentiate your program.

◆ **Description of Intended Audience.** Give a good laundry list of all the audiences for whom this project is being made. Provide demographic and psychographic information about whom you want to reach. Take a look at how filmmaker Arwen Lee Curry describes the target audience for her film *Worlds of Ursula K. Le Guin:*

TARGET AUDIENCE

Ursula K. Le Guin is a major American writer, with hundreds of thousands of loyal fans who will constitute a natural audience for the film. **Worlds of Ursula K. Le Guin** will also appeal to the vast community of sci-fi and fantasy fans, many of whom congregate virtually on blogs and spread "word of mouth" news at astounding rates. Because of the subject's popularity among technologically savvy groups, this project lends itself more than most to broadcast and distribution using new media. The producers will reach out to online gamers, Silicon Valley tech gurus, and comic book artists, as well as serious students (and professors) of philosophy, women's and gender studies, anthropology, political science, literature, or history.

Californians, born and naturalized, will be drawn to **Worlds of Ursula K. Le Guin**, which opens a new window on the state's history. Writers — working and aspiring — will want to know, as they always do, how such a prolific, successful writer works. Librarians and other community educators interested in increasing literacy and respect for the creative imagination will want to use the film as a tool to promote interest in the arts among their constituencies, which might include young children, adults, and seniors. For example, the film would lend itself well to writing workshops in senior centers or summer sessions for young adults.

Le Guin's popularity has spanned generations, and her work appeals to Americans in their twenties and thirties who are increasingly turning away from television and toward the arts, including literature and film, for in-depth news and cultural perspective. People who question our country's administration and actively consider alternatives to our current government are a natural audience. NPR listeners, readers of *Harper's* (where Le Guin regularly publishes), the *New Yorker,* the *New York Review of Books,* the *Atlantic Monthly,* the *Nation,* and other publications will take interest in the film.

In addition to these special groups, the producers will aim to spark the imagination of anyone who ever found themselves, as a young person, transported by a work of literature.

7. **Why I Became Involved With This Project**. A very brief — one or two sentences — explanation of how and why the filmmaker became involved with this project. This helps personalize the proposal, and answers any question the funder might have about the filmmaker's connection to the topic.

8. **Treatment**. For many funders, the treatment will be one of the most important sections of the entire proposal. I have had a number of funders tell me that this is where filmmakers often completely miss the mark. A treatment is very different from the description of the project earlier in the proposal. Instead, the treatment is literally a written depiction of exactly what will be seen in the project if a viewer were sitting in front of a screen — scene by scene. Everything in the treatment is visual, and there is no explanation of themes or intent. The formula the treatment follows is: "First we see... and then we see... and next we see...." Unless the funder says otherwise, try to keep the treatment to a length of two single-spaced pages.

Here is a segment of a treatment for the film *A Midwife's Life: Discovering the Life of Martha Ballard* by Laurie Kahn-Leavitt, which is reprinted from a full grant proposal with permission from the National Endowment for the Humanities:

It is the middle of the night. We are close on the face of a woman. It is streaked with sweat. The scene is claustrophobic, with faces, objects crowding the frame. The woman is groaning. The visual palette includes many rich shades of brown, lit by flickering yellow and red from the firelight. It is dark. We can almost smell the burning wood and the steam rising from the kettle in the fireplace. The presence of people in the room is magnified by long shadows cast against the unpainted wood walls of the house. We hear the voices of women talking, soothing the woman in labor, and the camera pulls back to reveal a scene filled with women — with their hands, shoulders, plain blouses, skirts. The woman in labor is not lying on a bed, but is squatting, in the final moments of childbirth, held in the arms of three other women. One rather older, somewhat stout, but strong woman is obviously in charge. Her face is plain, but the lines on her face and the look in her eyes reveal depth of character. She is giving instructions to the other women to get hot compresses, to rub the woman's lower back, to apply a specific herbal ointment. As she soothes and encourages the woman in labor, as the woman in labor pants and catches her breath, we hear the voice of the midwife reading an entry from her diary:

I was Calld to Capt Sualls wife in Travail I crost on the ice. Got there at 70 Clock Evenng. Mrs Sewalls neighbors were caild to her assistance. It was a very Cold night.

The midwife in charge leans over. And then we hear a loud baby's cry.

Mrs Sewall was safe delivered at 1 this morn of a fine daghter. May God long preserv her. I sett up with my Patients.

As the baby is cleaned off, wrapped, and eased into a wooden cradle, Tabitha Sewall names her daughter Elizabeth. She lies back in bed, exhausted from her nine-hour labor. The midwife and the three women who have helped out are drowsy. They lean back toward the kitchen fire, the midnight cold at their backs, small clouds of mist above their whispers.

◆ **Production Plans and Timeline.** Let the funder know where and when the project will be undertaken and what difficulties might be encountered. Place here a generic timeline for creating the film and taking it into distribution (as discussed in Chapter Three).

◆ **Personnel.** Provide brief, one-paragraph descriptions of each of the key personnel (yourself, the director, cinematographer, editor, advisors, etc.). Make sure everyone sounds credible, and be sure to mention major accomplishments and any significant awards.

◆ **Distribution Plans.** Describe all conceivable ways this program will reach its audience. This section must be very convincing. It must show that the filmmaker has really thought about and researched the various avenues of distribution.

Here is the distribution plan that filmmaker Tamara Perkins (Apple of Discord Productions), submitted with her application for the documentary *The Trust*:

The Trust has a multi-faceted distribution plan which leverages both new, innovative methods along with traditional routes of sales and release.

Educational Use
Inherent in the film project is the educational aspect as we bring this issue to underexposed audiences. An inmate-developed curriculum, Youth of Today, Leaders of Tomorrow, will be modified for use with different student audiences in High Schools, Colleges, and in Youth Development programs. Our relationships with Alameda County Public Health, Alameda County Probation, Oakland Unified School district, along with local Youth Development agencies such as YouthRadio, Youth Uprising, and The Mentoring Center will help facilitate the incorporation of the film and curriculum.

We will also lead a College Tour with panel and discussion. Our relationships with universities like the University of San Francisco, San Francisco State University, Stanford University, UC Davis, and UC Berkeley will help facilitate this tour. Our panel tour will begin with Dr. Kim Richman at the University of San Francisco, where we will address the systemic issues infusing the path to successful reentry to the Schools of Sociology, Criminal Science, Law, and Education.

Ellen Schneider, director of Active Voice (*activevoice.net*), is interested in a partnership to support the educational curriculum development and distribution. Her company is dedicated to putting a human face on public policy.

Grassroots Outreach
Community-based presentations, panel discussions, and forums have already begun and will continue in community centers, agency-led youth development forums, and local events, such as Berkeley's One Love People's Day in People's Park, as well as Day of Peace and Silence the Violence events held all over the Bay Area. We are also approaching Michael Franti's Power to the Peaceful event to showcase the trailer and host a community discussion at their annual September 11 event. East Bay Community Foundation is hosting a screening event focused on engaging and rallying the Bay Area Faith community behind the project. (*continues*)

(continued)

Screenings
Screenings will kick off at Google Headquarters in Mountain View. Screenings will also be held at the California College of the Arts and the Art Center College in L.A. Additional screenings will be held in New York and Washington, D.C.

Independent Distribution
Apple of Discord Productions is also a member of the Independent Feature Project (IFP) and is planning to attend New York's Independent Feature Project (IFP) September 14-19, 2008.

Cable Network & Public Television
Apple of Discord Productions has approached Oprah Winfrey Network (OWN) with *The Trust* documentary for airing after the festival and theatrical release.

On September 12, 2008, we received a strong letter of interest to distribute from KQED's Truly California executive producer, Sue Ellen McCann. We are also in talks with ITVS' Kathryn Washington regarding exploration of PBS as a partner in distribution of both the documentary and related works created by the San Quentin Media Project. Kathryn is opening a relationship with American Public Media and POV.

Film Festivals
We plan to circulate the movie through various national and international festivals, such as Sundance, LA International, IDFA Amsterdam, HotDocs, Silver Docs, Full Frame, and TrueFalse.

DVD Sales
In order to facilitate DVD sales beyond our own Web site, we will contract with Ironweed, Amazon Unboxed, and Netflix.

Web Sales and Streaming
As part of our alternative distribution plan we will be engaging services that allows users to discover, watch and share independent and world films online such as Jaman, Hulu, and Cacchi. We have also been approached by Link TV to share the trailer, and related media created by the San Quentin Media Project. Another Web-based alternative media we are utilizing is Current TV.

Social Networking
We will use several social networking sites to drive traffic to our site and promote both the production and distribution of the film. Sites already populated include: Facebook, LinkedIn, MySpace, Plaxo, and IndieGoGo.

Theatrical Release
Theatrical release opportunities will be researched for both Domestic and International distribution. Opportunities are being explored both through Independent Feature Project and through our relationship with The Doc Film Institute.

◆ **Community Outreach.** More and more, funders are interested in also seeing a community outreach plan — something that shows the filmmaker is concerned with partnerships that will help get the word out about the film and that will give added value to any broadcast. Many filmmakers will want to create a Web site for their projects. This is the part of the proposal where that Web site and how it extends the project can be described. Take a look at the community engagement scenario employed by the documentary *Race to Execution.* The film follows the haunting stories of two death row inmates, exposing the role race plays in who lives and who dies at the hands of the state. The film, produced and directed by Emmy Award–winner Rachel Lyon and co-produced by Jim Lopes, is a powerful documentary that enlarges the conversation regarding the death penalty, focusing attention to racial bias against black defendants that arise from unfair media coverage, race-of-jury and race-of-victim. Their community engagement plan takes all these assets, possibilities, and potential audiences into consideration:

RACE TO EXECUTION
COMMUNITY ENGAGEMENT CAMPAIGN PYRAMID

ჼg 2006

Funders & Thought Leaders. Got vision, feedback and key objectives from thought leaders at foundations and organizations with programmatic interest in criminal justice.

ჼmer 2006

Tested Ideas with Advocates. Once core objectives were determined, we met with key leaders in intersecting fields of criminal justice, racial justice, and law to identify possible outcomes, targets, framing, partners. etc. and determine ways to maximize upcoming broadcast.

ჼ06-Winter 07

Special Premieres and National Alliances. Organized strategic, high profile sneak previews w/ key allies including National Coalition to Abolish the Death Penalty, DePaul University College of Law and Applied Research Center. Began to develop alliances with national orgs to generate support for broadcast and upcoming campaign.

ჼh 2007

Independent Lens: Community Cinema and Broadcast. Worked with national criminal justice orgs to draw members and affiliates to local sneak previews (via ITVS' Community Cinema) and the broadcast. Panel discussions featured the filmmaker, attorneys, scholars, and former prisoners. Resources were developed, including web tools, discussion guides and a "what you can do" brochure for distribution at events. Worked to build list of interested viewers to keep them updated on the ongoing campaign.

ჼmer 2007

Reengage Thought Leaders & Identify New Opportunities. Convened braintrust meeting at the Ford Foundation to build on the success of broadcast and identify ways to reach "beyond the choir." Identified new target audiences beyond the criminal justice world: journalists, communities of faith and communities of color. Developed plan for post-broadcast campaign featuring new partners, a new online video module, a distribution database, revamped events, and a finale race and law symposium at DePaul University.

ჼ07- Spring 08

Post-Broadcast National Tour. Launched multi-city series of forums and screenings in partnership with churches, universities and journalism organizations. Customized events in each community to focus on local needs and objectives. Speakers included journalists of color, attorneys and former prisoners. Events were designed to spark greater awareness beyond the likely allies and inspire fairer and more accurate reporting of criminal justice issues. Premiered new video module, *Juror Number Six,* focused on media representation.

Distribution, Tools, Long Tail. Throughout, worked with filmmaker and national partners to create "framing" tools, event planning kit, and online resources that help viewers and users maximize impact of documentary. Worked to incorporate the video module and clips from the original film into online curriculum and online channels with groups such as Death Penalty Information Center and National Black Programming Consortium. Reengaged allies from pre-broadcast to alert interested viewers about new developments and spark interest in the video module.

◆ **Evaluation Plan.** The question of evaluation comes up because most of the projects' foundation support has clearly defined and quantifiable outcomes. Funders are increasingly sensitive to finding ways to measure the success of their funding efforts. Therefore, the question of evaluation is likely to come up and the filmmaker should be ready with an answer.

For many media projects the question may seem whimsical. How, for instance, can success be measured for a short experimental film, or for a dramatic feature that is meant to give people pleasure? Filmmakers need to be creative here and say they will make use of any or all of the following methods for evaluation:

- Measuring critical response in the media
- Response from specialists in the field
- Awards won at festivals
- Total number of sales in all intended markets
- Focus group opinions
- Evaluations from users
- Changes in behavior of the intended audience
- Amount of matching funds from various sources

◆ **Funding Strategy for Completion of Project.** Because most funders cannot provide full funding for a film project, there will be a portion of the budget that still must be raised over and above the request being made. Every funder will want to know how the filmmaker plans to raise the rest of the money. The key to providing a good answer is for the filmmaker to play "what if" and create a fundraising plan/strategy that actually sounds practical for the project. Here is a sample of how a strategy might look:

"We are requesting $50,000 from your foundation to begin production on our film *The Warshawski Family Diaries*, which has a total budget of $500,000. Should your foundation provide start-up costs, we plan to raise the remaining $450,000 in the following manner: 50% ($225,000) from donations from four or five private foundations and government agencies; 10% ($45,000) in pre-sales to foreign television; 20% ($90,000) from individuals through direct mail campaigns and fundraising houseparties; and 20% ($90,000) from corporate sponsors for a national airing on PBS."

◆ **Budgets.** I recommend having the following budgets ready to go:
  - A one-page budget summary that shows the major headings and subtotals
  - A complete budget for the entire project that shows detail for every expense and is heavily annotated with as many budget notes as necessary
  - Separate detailed budgets for various "projects" — those portions of the entire film for which you are planning to request support (e.g. script development, community outreach, post-production, etc.)

◆ **Fiscal Sponsor Letter.** Funders will need to see a copy of the fiscal sponsors official 501(c)(3) letter provided by the IRS, which proves their nonprofit status. In addition to this, ask the fiscal sponsor to write an enthusiastic "to whom it may concern" cover letter that explains why they decided to sponsor the project, and why they feel it is important that funders provide support. Also keep on file brochures and promotional materials about the fiscal sponsor just in case the sponsor might be unfamiliar to the funder.

◆ **Letters of Support.** Garnering letters of support should be a part of every filmmaker's *modus operandi*. These letters are especially important in helping to gain credibility for a filmmaker and a project when asking for grants. Start getting letters as soon as possible from:
  - Professional associations and experts in the topic area of the film
  - Other well-known and well-respected filmmakers in the genre of the film
  - Distributors (these are the strongest letters that can be attached to a grant)
  - Broadcasters
  - Potential end-users

Make sure the letter is written on letterhead stationery, contains no typos, and is signed. Do not be surprised if a potential supporter when asked for a letter says: "I'm happy to give you a letter, but I'm not sure what to say. Would you mind writing it for me and I'll have it typed up on my stationery?" I love it when I am asked to write my own letter of reference because now I can be sure to get the exact letter I want and need.

- **Letters of Commitment.** Keep these on file to keep yourself safe. Make sure that anyone and everyone mentioned by name in the proposal as a participant in the film has written an official note for the files that confirms commitment to the project. This is especially important when well-known people are being attached to a project. Funders will want to know that the filmmaker is not just name-dropping.

- **Press Clippings.** Generate as much press coverage as possible about both the project and the production team. Press clippings are a great boon to the credibility of the filmmaker — even if the source is a hometown newspaper. Clippings help lay the groundwork for fundraising by raising awareness of the project and helping to generate "buzz." Learn the fine art of photocopying and make sure that all press clippings meet the following criteria:

- Clean, crisp, legible copies — both paper and electronic versions
- For hard copies: Original-size copies (never reduce the clipping to a smaller type size). Longer articles cam be cut up and laid out on a series of 8 ½" by 11" sheets of plain white paper
- Each clipping contains a contact name and address
- Each clipping provides the name of the original source, date of publication, and page numbers

If the mention of the team and the project are just a small part of a larger article, then excerpt just that portion, or highlight that part with a marker, or bring attention to that portion by increasing its size and placing the drawing of a magnifying glass around it.

- **Full Résumés of Personnel.** Have all team members and advisors provide a full résumé to keep on file. These can be excerpted for use in grants. Occasionally a funder will want to see a full résumé.

◆ **Demo Reel/Trailer.** It is possible to begin a project and not have a promo clip of the intended work. However, once some funds have been accrued and some shooting has taken place, almost every funder will request a look at some work in progress that represents the tenor of the film and shows the skills of the team. The demo reel does not have to be long — anything from three to ten minutes is usually enough. I do not recommend longer samples because it shows the funder too much, and leaves open too many opportunities to make mistakes and/ or trigger too many new questions. Short and sweet is just fine.

Having said that, I do have two other criteria for the effective fundraising clip. The first is that the content of the clip should (ideally) be very representative of the style and content of the intended finished film, and that it should be very engaging. The clip should make the viewer want to see more.

My second criterion is one that filmmakers do not like to hear — the clip should be as technically "clean" and free of problems (sound and image) as possible. Funders — even very seasoned and media-savvy ones — have difficulty seeing beyond technical difficulties in a tape. This means that the filmmaker is going to have to spend some time and money creating a good clean copy of some material. Do not think that an explanatory note can be attached to a tape and that will take care of any problems. Here is a sample of an actual note that a filmmaker sent me to accompany a sample reel:

> **PLEASE NOTE** that the material found on this tape consists of excerpted scenes, *not* examples of completed work. As such, it is important to keep in mind several things while viewing:
>
> - You are viewing 16mm film work print that has been transferred to videotape. In the final version, the color will be corrected and a clean print created.
>
> - The narration you hear is *temporary* and rough, and is read by an amateur. The final narration will emphasize goal-action-results messages and will refer to specific principles of creating community change. In the final version it will be read by a professional narrator.

- Scenes do not flow as smoothly as they will in the final version. Some shots will be replaced.

- The sounds levels are uneven. Voices will be much clearer in final version. Scenes with no sound at all will be filled with sound effects or music. The music is also temporary, although evocative of what we intend.

- At this stage, there are no titles or name identifiers for the people speaking.

If the work sample needs to have this type of note attached to it, then the video is not ready to be sent out at all. These notes are rarely read by funders, and when they are read are often ignored the moment an image comes on the screen.

Occasionally the filmmaker will not have new material to submit from the intended project, and may want to create a sample reel of past work. This work might also include samples from completed pieces by other team members (especially the cinematographer and the editor). In this case, try to include works that are as similar to the intended project as possible. It would be a mistake, for instance, to submit a vérité documentary sample for a dramatic narrative feature proposal.

One last instruction is to only send a sample when a funder gives permission or makes a specific request. Also submit the sample in the format the funder wants, label and package the sample appropriately, and be sure to include a self-addressed stamped envelope if return of the work is desired.

The following is some sage advice from DocuDoctor Fernanda Rossi:

TEN TIPS FOR
GREAT FUNDRAISING SAMPLES

1. No matter what people in the film business call them — whether demo, sample, trailer, taster or sizzler; **the function is more important than the name** — think of it as an *audiovisual pitch for fundraising*, and throw away the dictionary.

2. **The demo needs to be consistent in content and style with the rest of your materials:** written proposal and pitch. If the synopsis says *an experimental documentary*, the sample has to support that statement.

3. **A marketing trailer is very different than a fundraising demo.** The first needs to convince hundreds of people to spend 90 minutes and $1. The second needs to persuade very few people to spend several years with you and many thousands on your project. Quite a different challenge! That's why:

4. **A fundraising trailer is not a "movie preview meets music video"** — it's actually more like a short without an ending.

5. **The opening of a fundraising demo does not need the elements of the opening of the actual documentary** — no long credits, long pans, moody slow scenes — get to the point in the first minute without delays.

6. **A fundraising trailer should have complete scenes as opposed to a fast cut assortment of provocative sound bites and images.** The purpose of a demo is to convey the essential points of your story. A flashy choppy teaser only conveys that you can afford a fancy editor and graphic designer — not that you're a good storyteller or that there is a story to tell.

7. **Stay away from montages or scenes cut to music.** Also avoid music and/or narration from beginning to end. In general those elements are used when a story doesn't work well on its own.

8. **Slates with explanatory text and fades to black are not as necessary as you might think.** In general they disrupt the flow and momentum of the story. Delay including them until there is no other option.

9. **A demo must have a cliffhanger or hook at the end** that hints there is more to the story than what it was shown so far. If the trailer gives closure, making it work just fine as a short, why would anybody bother to invest time and money in a longer piece?

10. **A cliffhanger can create great expectations.** Do not kill that emotional high by adding final credits or contact info such as telephone numbers or e-mail address. Let your prospective audience be thrilled and enthusiastic until they press stop in their player. They can always look in the DVD case for your contact info.

Internationally renowned speaker, author and story consultant Fernanda Rossi has doctored over 200 documentaries and fundraising trailers including the 2007 Academy Award® nominated *Recycled Life* by Leslie Iwerks. She is the author of the book *Trailer Mechanics: A Guide to Making Your Documentary Fundraising Trailer.* You can find Fernanda at *www.documentarydoctor.com.*

LAST CALLS

Now that the proposal has been sent in (well before the official deadline), it may seem that the filmmaker's work is done. Not true. There is still one more very crucial phone call that must be made. One last window of opportunity remains for the filmmaker to help increase chances of success. A week or two after submitting the grant, call the program officer in charge of the proposal and ask if the paperwork arrived safely, if the officer has had a chance to look it over, and if there are any questions the officer would like to ask.

It is amazing how often a grant is submitted with small or even large errors. I once looked over a proposal about to be submitted to the Corporation for Public Broadcasting (CPB) for $500,000, and right on the cover page the filmmaker had made an addition error. It is not the job of the foundation to call applicants back and advise them of errors in a proposal. However, if the filmmaker makes the call to a sympathetic program officer, quite often that person will allow corrections to be made to any mistakes or any confusing narrative portions before the grant is given to the deciding panel or board of trustees. Many a grant can be won or lost as a result of this call.

The very first time I ever offered my workshop on fundraising I gave this advice to the participants: "If any of you have submitted a grant recently and it is still pending, go home and call the program officer right away to see if everything is okay." A few weeks later I got a call from a woman who attended the workshop and wanted to tell me that this suggestion was the most important thing she had learned. The day after the workshop she called the foundation where she had submitted a grant for her documentary. The program officer told her he was glad she had called because there was a section of her proposal that he did not quite understand and he wondered if she could give him a better explanation. The filmmaker described over the phone what she had meant, and the program officer replied, "Oh, that makes much more sense. Our board doesn't meet for another two weeks, so why don't you rewrite that section of the grant just as you told it to me over the phone, and I'll substitute it for what you sent me." She ended up getting the grant she requested and was certain this change had made all the difference.

Once this call is made, the rest is up to the funder. After the board of trustees meets, the funder will contact all applicants, usually in writing. Some few lucky applicants will receive a "Congratulations, You Won!" letter. When this happens, be sure to say "thank you" to the funder and to the program officer who was the main contact. A simple card or phone call will suffice. Do not forget to ask funders if they want to be formally mentioned in the film's credits and publicity (some will want to remain anonymous), and if they have a particular wording or image they prefer to have used. And, make sure to stay in touch with your funders throughout the progress of the production, to invite them to an opening screening when the film is complete, and to send them a copy of the program for their files. The funder has now become your partner and will want to be treated like a team member.

Many more applicants are going to receive a "Sorry, Pardner, You Lose" rejection letter. These letters typically are written in a generalized way that goes something like:

> "Dear Applicant: Thank you for bringing your project to our foundation for consideration. Our board of trustees has just met and it is my unfortunate task to have to tell you that your project was not chosen for support this year. Although we found your project of great interest, we are just not able to help all the fine applicants like yourself that come to our foundation for assistance each year. We wish you the best of luck with your endeavors, and invite you to apply to us again in the future should you have a project that closely matches our guidelines."

These rejection letters rarely, if ever, tell the specific reasons for rejection. Therefore, the filmmaker still has one more call to make. Make sure the anger and depression caused by rejection has subsided before making this call. Then pick up the phone and contact the program officer at the foundation. Be very polite. Thank the foundation for having taken time to consider the application you sent. Then directly ask the program officer if she could be kind enough to provide a little more detail on the discussion that took place during the consideration of the proposal, and if there is any important information that she can give you about the reasons for being rejected. Never ever get angry with the funder, or berate them for not giving support.

I remember once giving this advice to a filmmaker who immediately said, "I tried that once and it didn't work!" I asked him to explain what happened and he said, "Well, I got a standard rejection letter from a foundation that really should have given me a grant and I was really pissed. My film was exactly within their mission and guidelines and they had no good reason for rejecting me. So I called up the program officer at the foundation and complained. I told her that they were wrong not to give me the grant, and that they obviously had not looked at it closely, and that I wanted to send it back to them so they could reconsider." This is a perfect example of how you should *never* talk to a funder. This filmmaker ruined his chances for ever getting a grant from this foundation, and he tainted the waters for other filmmakers as well. No one likes to get rejected, but you have to learn how to handle these rejections professionally.

If the application went to a government funder, then they must divulge notes from the panel meeting and give some good solid reasons for the rejection. Private foundation officers are not under the same obligation to divulge information, but quite often they can provide details that might be very revealing. Perhaps the filmmaker is doing something in the application that confuses funders. Or maybe the funder only said "no" because it is the end of the fiscal year and they had no funds left over. Whatever the reason, the filmmaker has to make an effort to ferret it out. Also, the filmmaker when making this call is sending a very strong signal to the funding community. That signal says: "I am serious about this endeavor. Every time I am rejected I will be making this phone call." Funders will take the filmmaker more seriously, and tend to pay more attention to the next application for support.

Even with funders that have rejected a proposal, I would counsel to stay in touch. Keep them informed on the progress of the project (via press releases and newsletters), and be sure they hear about the successful completion of the film and are invited to an opening screening. This helps lay the groundwork for any future proposals. Fundraising from foundations is a long-term process, so consider any rejection a short-term loss that provides an opportunity for eventual long-term gain.

By the time a proposal is accepted, the funder and the filmmaker have engaged in a delicate courtship. Active Voice, a media strategy company that frequently works as an intermediary between people with money and people with cameras, has learned that both funders and filmmakers need language and guidelines so these partnerships can thrive. Active Voice suggests that "prenups" can help all parties understand each other's goals, professional standards, and value systems before they "tie the knot."

Prenup Guidelines:
HELPING FILMMAKERS AND
FUNDERS SEE "EYE TO EYE"

Dramatic changes in media and philanthropy have spawned many new ways in which filmmakers and funders might work together. Many "engaged" grant makers are seeing the need for powerful films that advance change efforts. Filmmakers want to tell stories that have an impact in the public square. But as interaction between funders and filmmakers increases, so too does the potential for misunderstandings. Here are just a few items filmmakers and funders can think about and discuss:

- **Are You Right for Each Other?**
We didn't choose the term "prenups" accidentally. Are you a good match? Do you share a vision for the film's approach and impact? Have you discussed what you're getting into? Do you trust each other?

- **Yours? Mine? Ours?**
Who owns the copyright? The answer may seem obvious, but this issue is often ignored when media grants are made, maybe because many independent filmmakers assume that they automatically own the copyright. Many newer funders think that if they paid for a film, the copyright is theirs. Can the funder's other grantees have free copies? Should the film be "open source"? (One filmmaker we know was surprised to see offers for free copies of her independent film on her funder's website.)

- **Getting Involved**
Creative control is one of the most contentious issues in relationships between filmmakers and funders. Filmmakers often want complete independence in telling the story. And funders, if they're going to make a large grant, often want a film that will be in keeping with their program goals. Does the funder expect to review rough cuts? What's the process for feedback? Must the filmmaker accept suggestions? *(continues)*

Prenup Guidelines (cont.)

• **It'll Have a Happy Ending... Right?**

Sometimes a story takes a dramatic twist that changes the focus of the film. A main character or featured institution might have a change of heart, drop out, or even protest the production or the distribution. The film might contain perspectives that the funder or stakeholders reject. Or maybe the funder just doesn't like the finished product. What language can be included in a prenup to handle the unexpected turns that are inevitable in "real life"?

Ellen Schneider, Executive Director, Active Voice
Jon Funabiki, Professor of Journalism, San Francisco State University
For more information, visit *www.activevoice.net*

CHAPTER SIX

ALL THE REST

*"Blessed are the flexible, for they
shall not be bent out of shape."*
— Michael McGriffy, M.D.

ALTERNATIVE STRATEGIES

Filmmakers can be very creative about finding support. Thinking "outside the box" can unearth some interesting new ways to fund your film.

Earlier I mentioned the luck Josh Caldwell and Hunter Weeks had raising corporate support for their documentaries. For their film *10 MPH* they employed a novel distribution strategy. They made the entire film available for free on YouTube. The film was preceded by a short message from Weeks, who explained that if viewers signed up to be members of an entertainment Web site called *OurStage. com*, the filmmakers would receive $1, and that viewers who signed up would also get a free iPod download of the film. That brought in a little over $10,000.

Tiffany Shlain (*www.tiffanyshlain.com*) is an award-winning filmmaker (*The Tribe* and *Life, Liberty & the Pursuit of Happiness*) who knows her way around the Web. She is founder of The Webby Awards, co-founder of the International Academy of Digital Arts and Sciences and director of The Moxie Institute. Tiffany believes that "artists should be able to earn a living doing what they love. As a filmmaker, there is a lot of low-hanging technological fruit to help make that happen." Here is some of her sage advice:

TIFFANY'S TECHNO TIPS

- **Put your website URL in your film credits** with a specific note that people can buy your film there.

- **Find a fulfillment house** to send your DVDs out once you make a sale, and charge the buyer the shipping and handling fees. We use a great place called Video Transform in Palo Alto.

- **Think of Withoutabox.com as the indie filmmaker's theatrical roll-out**. Enter as many festivals as possible. Each of these festivals has gathered a fantastic audience to view your work. Make the most of these screenings by distributing flyers that tell people where they can buy your films.

- **Always gather e-mail addresses at every screening you have**. These people are your community; they will help you to continue to get the word out. Be sure also to get their zip codes, so that you can alert them when you are having another screening in their areas. We use the e-mail service Vertical Response to manage our e-mail lists.

- **Create a simple, easily updated website** through iWeb or some other out-of-the-box updatable web tools. It does not need to be complicated, but should include basic information on your film, a trailer, and a link to where people can buy your film. Keep the content fresh with a blog that updates audiences on the progress of the film. I recommend starting the site while the film is in production so that you have an engaged audience that is ready to see the film when it is finished.

- **Experiment with posting your films to film websites**. Sites like iTunes, YouTube, Jaman, IndieGoGo generally reach different demographics, and will help you to expand your audience. Right now it is all about throwing the spaghetti against the online world and seeing what works.

One aspiring Canadian filmmaker, Casey Walker, launched a Web site where he sold frames of his yet-to-be-made film at $10 each. In return, investors received a credit in the movie, advertisement rights on his site, and a cut of the profits if the film made money. If the film is successful, investors will get 50% of the profits based on the number of frames they purchased, while the other half goes to pay the production company, cast and crew. The last time I looked he had raised $180,000, which included me as one of his one-frame investors!

From *http://mymilliondollarmovie.com/index-en.php*, used by permission. Photo by Marc Duchemin.

Mike Shiley is an independent producer/director who has earned over $1million from his three top films. He's best known for creating the documentaries *Inside Iraq* and *Dark Water Rising*. Here is a letter I got from Mike talking about how he funds his work:

> I self-finance all my own films and find income-producing opportunities while in the field on a shoot. I own prosumer equipment (camera, still, tripod and mics). I use frequent flier miles to fly, volunteer field producers (I just pay their expenses), and do the editing myself on Final Cut Pro on my laptop. Because I get fees to screen, which are arranged in advance by my agent, I know before I start shooting that my film will be profitable! I have never spent more than $5,000 on any one film.

When I was in Iraq, I was embedded with the US military, so it cost me nothing. Also, while in Iraq, I sold still photos of soldiers to their respective home newspapers for $150 a shot and video footage of units to their home local news affiliate stations for $1,000 an hour. I also sold some captured footage of an Apache helicopter shooting Iraqi civilians to ABC News for $5,000. All in all, I made about $10,000 selling footage, stills and video while on location, which meant that I came home with a net profit of $5,000 and a film in the can! Not bad...

The second time I went to Iraq, I went in with a local Portland NGO (Northwest Medical Teams International) group as a private freelance journalist. In exchange for room, board and an entrée into Iraq, I gave them photos, video and some copy writing that they used to update the media and leverage into over $5 million in donations. They wound up paying me $1,000 because they were happy with my work. NGOs always need help in marketing with good stills, video and copywriting. All local news outlets love stories of their citizens doing work overseas (especially in the military) and will pay on the spot for the artwork.

When I returned, I sold my footage through a royalty-free stock footage site (*www.DVArchive.com*), where I have made about $10,000 over the years, which also has helped out a lot.

When I was traveling through Serbia, I bumped into a *Wall Street Journal* reporter on the train who introduced me to CNN at the hotel. They needed a still photographer to travel with them, as theirs missed the flight from New York, so I worked for $65 a day traveling through the former Yugoslavia, into Kosovo and Bosnia during the 1993 war (*Siege of Sarajevo*). I photographed Kosovo before it blew up into the ethnic cleansing atrocities by the Serbs. I even got to meet the future war criminal and, at the time, current president of Yugoslavia, Slobodan Milosevic. I worked for 15 days with the CNN crew and made almost $1,000. Not to mention being a part of history and the memories and stories that will last a lifetime!

I think if filmmakers are going to shoot in hot spots and/or use HD cameras, there is a big market for stock and royalty-free markets, as well as the sources I listed above.

So it's not all about getting grants and going down the traditional roads of financing. Filmmakers can use their talents, crews and equipment in the field to earn money to finance their films.

Best,

Mike Shiley, Producer/Director

Shidog Films

mike@shidogfilms.com

Arin Crumley and Susan Buice — producers, directors, and stars of their 71-minute indie feature *Four Eyed Monsters* (www. foureyedmonsters.com) — pursued a number of nontraditional fundraising and distribution strategies. They became the first filmmakers to have a feature-length film featured on YouTube. They took advantage of the opportunity by partnering with the then-new website Spout.com, which offered the filmmakers $1 for each new registrant that came to Spout.com as a result of the offer on YouTube (with a cap of $100,000). The filmmakers made $3,500 in the first 24 hours, and eventually raised $50,000 this way. To date, over one million people have viewed their film on YouTube.

Let's end this section with some sage advice on new alternative fundraising methods from Wendy Levy, Director of Creative Programming and the Producers Institute for New Media Technologies at Bay Area Video Coalition in San Francisco:

WENDY LEVY'S ALTERNATIVE WAYS TO RAISE MONEY FOR MEDIA PROJECTS

Engage Your Audience First/Strategic Modes of Engagement

In traditional financing and distribution models, audience members are the last customers to the table. Shake up this paradigm! If you identify your primary audience first (and remember that they are not just your viewers, but also your collaborators and partners), put some short, enticing, high-quality content online that they can sink their teeth into and share widely, and provide an easy-to-access tool for online charitable donations (for example, *www.reelchanges.org* or *www.indiegogo.com*), **they will help you fundraise** in so many important ways. They can:

- give you money and get their friends to give you money
- scale traffic to your Web site so you can leverage ad dollars
- increase awareness of your project with strategic funders and community organizations
- create and participate in a network of audience members who can help you and want to be involved

Join with Strategic Organizations Early/Collaborative Fundraising

Partner up as early as possible with organizations that serve the people and communities your story is about. Stories inspire movements, and movements make change happen. You need to incent and scale public interest in your project early in the process — let your stakeholders in and let them participate! Have a fundraiser with an organization with hundreds or thousands of members and SHARE the proceeds. Through collaborative fundraising, you get to align yourself with your issue and collect e-mails of like-minded people who can give you more down the road. Your best and most dynamic organizational partners might collaborate on grants as well — with your film being a cornerstone of a community development, environmental, or social justice initiative.

Make the News/Blogging for Dollars

Bloggers can be your biggest allies in fundraising for issue-driven media projects. Identify the respected, high-profile bloggers with dedicated readerships and engage them in the newsworthy aspects of your project. Save special, unique content for your best blogger-partners — their coverage can potentially drive major traffic to your site, where your job is to engage them, keep them coming back, and inspire them to participate. Your project should have its own blog as well — done right, this will raise awareness around the urgency of the project, develop a community around your work, and allow you to scale your audience while you are still shooting and editing.

(continues)

ALTERNATIVE WAYS TO RAISE MONEY FOR MEDIA PROJECTS (cont.)

Explore Multiple Platforms/Any Time, Anywhere Fundraising

Just as we are in an era of any time-anywhere media consumption (we all agree by this point that appointment television is over), you might want to think about fundraising this way too. If you want to change the world, you have to play with it first. Do you know a flash developer who can skin a short, casual game that explores issues in your film? End each game with a link to your site, and build action items into game play. Radio is a platform that is so old school, it's new school. Create a series of high-quality podcasts about your subject and your film, and upload them to the Public Radio Exchange (*www.prx.org*). Pitch the stories to your local public radio station. Your story, the urgency of the issue, and your unique voice will create donors out of audience members who hear the program. Use your social networks for the Cause: give your Facebook friends a cool-looking widget, a fantastic video to share, a donation link to distribute, and they will do it.

Wendy Levy, Director
Creative Programming and the Producers Institute for
New Media Technologies
Bay Area Video Coalition, San Francisco

STUDENTS

I get many requests from undergraduate and graduate students asking how to raise support for their short film or thesis project. Unfortunately, I cannot be very encouraging for filmmakers in formal training programs who need money for their projects. Most foundations and government agencies have little or no interest at all in supporting the creation of student-made films. The exceptions might be those funders who have a vested interested in media education, but those are few and far between. Students generally will have to rely on scholarships and financial support available through their educational institutions.

If a student is serious about finding donations, then the best route would be to approach individuals — especially relatives. Throwing a fundraising houseparty or two might be appropriate. One creative solution that I heard involved a young filmmaker who sold shares in his future! The graduate student filmmaker made a promise to everyone who gave him funds to finish his thesis film: When he became a professional filmmaker and started making commercial films, they all would receive a small percentage of all his future profits.

Another common query I receive from students is if I know anyone who will just give them the equipment they need to make their films. The answer here, again, is probably "no." Funders shy away from giving money for the purchase of equipment, and manufacturers rarely will donate equipment. Entrepreneurial young filmmakers will, like their older cohorts, find ways to get access to the production and postproduction tools at either low or no cost, and then purchase the tools they need as their careers progress.

Here is a case study of a student film and how it successfully cobbled together $60,000 from:

◆ equity investors
◆ a donor who wanted to be on the set
◆ friends and family
◆ a student loan
◆ vendor discounts

Film: *The Abbatoir*
Type: Short, student film
Total Cost: About $60,000
Funding: Awards, private investors, friends and family, vendor discounts, self-funding, student loan

TJ Volgare was a graduate film student at University of Southern California when he finished the script for his short film, *The Abbatoir,* about a young man who is forced to confront the violence of his past when he returns home after being expelled from the Marines.

He had made short films before, which he had self-funded, but *The Abbatoir* was a much larger project, so he began his search for funding through grant research. But, after sorting through more than 200 grants, he found *The Abbatoir,* being a short, student film, wasn't eligible for a vast majority of the grants available to filmmakers.

In the meantime, Volgare had applied for several awards, including the Jeff Jones Award that he won through the USC scholarship committee for his script, which granted him $6,000, and the Panavision New Filmmaker Award, which gave him a reduced rate on a Panavision camera.

(continues)

The next step in the funding of *The Abattoir* came in the form of two private investors. The first came from Crystal Springs Productions in L.A., who they connected with through a close friend. "They read the script and thought the themes were timely and important," Volgare said. "And they saw it as a good foundation for some feature films to come."

The Abbatoir (cont.)

The other investor came from a client of one of the film's collaborators, who was interested in making a donation. In exchange, they brought him on set and involved him in every aspect of the film. "He just saw us as a bunch of young, purpose-driven artists trying to tell a story," he said.

Combined with some donations from friends and family and $2,000 taken from part of a student loan, they had the foundation of their funding secured and Volgare and his crew began to develop their idea further, planning out how the film was going to play out visually, and creating a statement on why they wanted to make the film. They combined that with the crew bios and a list of projects they had planned for the future, which helped them sell their idea to vendors, like Fuji Film, that gave them discounts on equipment.

He said the effort they put into packaging the idea and using the film as a foundation for their greater aspirations is what convinced vendors to invest in, not only the film, but the talents and ambitions of the filmmakers. "As a student, most vendors will give you a good rate," Volgare said. "It's important to ask… Especially if you're doing something experimental because the people providing you with the product can benefit from these experiments. Plus, there are advantages to developing relationships with filmmakers early on, which is what these vendors tried to do… but, most of these vendors just want to see the students succeed."

Utilizing his past experiences in stretching a budget, Volgare was able to go a long way with his limited budget. "I knew in what ways I didn't need to be excessive," he said.

In all, it took Volgare and his crew ten months to raise the funds needed to make *The Abattoir* and, though he admits it was a lot of work, it is something he strongly recommends to filmmakers in his position, especially student filmmakers. "It's a good skill to learn early on," he said. "It's good practice for what you're going to be doing as a feature filmmaker. And maybe it will offer us some credit as artists and managers of resources."

The Abattoir has screened at the New Orleans Film Festival and at the New Hampshire Film Festival. Volgare hopes the film will serve as a companion to feature scripts that he is currently working on.

(This case study was written by Nikki Chase and appeared in *The Independent*, a publication of Independent Media Publications, www.independent-magazine.org.)

GOING CORPORATE

My clients have not had great success getting donations from large corporations that do not have a formal foundation. Most corporations tend to shun controversy and are conservative in their funding choices. This stance eliminates alliances with many of the film topics chosen by independent filmmakers. Also, the corporate world is one fundraising environment where having connections does make a significant difference, and most independent filmmakers are not "connected."

However, it is possible to get support from corporations. The filmmaker who follows this path must keep in mind one major difference between corporations and all other funders: A corporation will always want something in return for its donation, and that something is almost always exposure with a specific audience (e.g., potential or current customers for the corporation's products). This principle is often referred to as "Enlightened Self Interest" or **ESI**.

This means that in addition to the written materials required for a full grant proposal to a foundation, the filmmaker must also be prepared to be lucid on two more issues:

- ◆ **Specific demographics of the intended audience.** The corporation will want to see facts and figures for exactly whom the program will reach, where they live, and how many people will end up viewing the program in what settings. Be prepared to have this data for every market the program will enter during distribution.
- ◆ **What's in it for them.** Opportunities for exposure need to be enumerated. Where will the corporation's name/logo appear in the film, in its packaging, and in promotional materials? What kind of community outreach and marketing/PR will be done, and how prominent will the filmmakers display the corporation's level of involvement? Are there ways the corporation can use the program internally with its staff, or with its clients, as a promotional tool or as a perk for employees?

The corporation is going to take the figures provided, do the math (e.g., total cost of its investment divided by total number of potential viewers), and come up with a figure for how much it will cost to reach each person using the film as a vehicle. If this figure does not compare favorably with normal costs of advertising, then it will not make sense to be involved with the film.

It is not unusual to have a list of "sponsorship opportunities" with different levels of support at which the corporation receives different benefits. All this means is that when the filmmaker talks to the corporation, the conversation has a different tone and flavor to it than the conversation with a foundation program officer or an individual donor. The filmmaker has to be prepared to convince the corporation that the film is a great marketing opportunity and an excellent vehicle for gaining goodwill in the community or in the work place.

There are exceptions to these rules for corporations. Funding at a corporation is very personality based — and that personality is generally whoever is running the business. When a CEO has a personal interest in a topic or in a filmmaker, then a donation can be made on that basis alone. Filmmaker Jon Else, for instance, was able to get support from The Gap for his documentary *Cadillac Desert* because "the guy who owns The Gap is a resolute environmentalist ... he's also a guy who's very resolute about giving something back to the community." (*RealScreen*, January 1998). It is a smart idea to keep up on CEOs by reading the business sections and society columns of newspapers, and keeping tabs on their Web sites. If you discover a corporate leader who has shown some personal interest in the same topic as your film, then anything can happen. The trick will be to reach that person, ideally through finding an intermediary who can open the door for the filmmaker, or at the very least through writing an introductory letter.

Ann Telfer, Director of *In Love and In Danger: A Documentary on Dating Violence,* literally ran into her connection to the corporation Parke-Davis (now Pfizer) on the track at a recreation center in Ann Arbor, Michigan. Her running mate, whose husband was the Chief Financial Officer at Parke-Davis, helped open the door to a meeting with the Vice President of the Human Resources Department, which resulted in a $30,000 donation. Telfer had done her research and knew something about the VP, as well as what the HR Department does. She pitched her project emphasizing the angle of domestic violence and the work force — an issue of interest to Parke-Davis. After this initial donation, Telfer maintained an eight-year relation, with lots of dialogue, that resulted in funding for a second tape, as well as a donation to fund a Dating and Domestic Violence Prevention Endowment.

Hunter Weeks (*www.hunterweeks.com*) is an independent filmmaker (*10 MPH, 10 Yards, Ride the Divide*) who has been very successful at getting corporate sponsorship support. "My first three films were made possible in part by generous support (not just free product, but cold, hard cash) from companies like Quiznos, Crocs, SmartWool, and CBS Sports. Many filmmakers I've met either think it's impossible to get corporate support or ethically wrong. I say it's not that difficult and easy to preserve your ethical integrity," says Weeks. Here are ten great tips from Hunter:

HOW TO GET COMPANIES TO HELP FUND YOUR FILM

1. **Think Partnership.** Which companies or organizations are trying to reach a similar audience? You need to be able to prove that your movie speaks to the same demographic that they are spending millions of dollars trying to reach.

2. **Find Your Person.** Google search for the VP or Director of Marketing or a PR person. Often you can find a good person's contact info on a press release. PR people know how valuable it can be to hook up with a movie. Also, think about social networking tools like LinkedIn, Facebook, Twitter. Remember, you're seeking out a real person who will understand the value of creating a partnership/sponsorship with your film for their company. Don't be afraid to call the general switchboard at Frito-Lay and ask who you would speak to about a co-promotional opportunity regarding a feature-length film. Sometimes it takes multiple tries to get to the right person.

3. **Meet in Person.** If at all possible, try to arrange a meeting in person. Most major metropolitan cities have many major brands with corporate headquarters. I've had the most success with companies based in the Denver area where I live.

4. **Stand Out.** Marketing executives and PR people deal with all kinds of proposals to bring exposure to their products and services. Be unique, confident, and assertive.

(continues)

HOW TO GET COMPANIES
TO HELP FUND YOUR FILM (cont.)

5. **Distribution vs. Product Placement.** Product placement is great, but if you don't believe in it, no problem. You'll have much better luck getting money if you convey how many impressions the brand or product will get through your distribution efforts. Think Web site, "presented by" message, trailer, film festivals, screenings, theatrical tour, press releases, DVD extras, your interviews, social networking. There are so many ways you can provide exposure and that's what these companies are after — just like you are with your film. Get them eyeballs.

6. **Make Pitch Short, Sweet, and Simple.** The first way to not get a deal is to burn yourself out on creating a pitch document. Keep it short (one or two pages) and make it look great.

7. **Excite with Examples of Success.** This should seem obvious, but don't overlook the sheep-like qualities that most marketers have. They don't innovate. They look at other stellar examples of success.

8. **Follow Up — More Than Once.** The people you are pitching are busy and unless you keep after them, you'll soon be forgotten. It's a sales process.

9. **Think About Online Video.** Marketers are really struggling because conventional advertising is failing them. TV ads don't work, so everyone is looking online for ways to capture their audiences. Why not create exclusive content (a series or just a clip or two) that coincides with the release of your film?

10. **Hook Up with Pros.** If this is your first film, find a way to get some professional filmmakers with extensive experience on board — network, visit their Web sites, check out places like *workbookproject .com*. Going into these meetings with experience and DVD copies of previous work to lay on the table goes a long way. Don't be too green when you are trying to get the greenbacks.

THE CORNER STORE

Small businesses can be an excellent source of support, especially for small and mid-sized projects that have any type of community setting. Because small business owners and operators are besieged by requests for donations, many have a policy of not giving money. They are afraid that word will spread and then they will be obliged to write checks to everyone in the community who knocks on their door. Small businesses are much more likely to donate goods and services.

The great thing about small-business fundraising is that these businesses are so easy to approach, and so little paperwork is needed. The filmmaker can literally walk around the neighborhood and speak directly with business owners. Often the only paperwork that is needed is a simple one or two-page write-up about the project, the crew, and what the business will receive in return for giving support. It helps if you can have some written support from someone important in the community — a politician, media personality, editor of the local newspaper, principal of the high school. If you're having trouble deciding which businesses to approach, visit the local Chamber of Commerce and ask for suggestions.

A filmmaker I knew was working on a project that included student interns. Together they canvassed the neighborhood where the shoot would take place. Letters were sent in advance letting business owners know that the team would be contacting them. The letters included a list of the items needed by the film. After walking around and making their personal solicitations, the team was able to secure a number of goods and services that made a tremendous difference to the project, including free lunches for the crew, free photocopies of the scripts, and free use of cell phones during production. In return for support, the small businesses were mentioned in the end credits of the film and in all press releases. Other things that can be offered in thanks include guest appearance in the film as an extra; free and/or reduced-cost copies of the film; placement of the business logo on posters, T-shirts, and on film packaging; invitation to and prominent recognition at the local premiere and/ or cast wrap party.

GOOD HOUSEKEEPING

By now it should be clear that fundraising can be a complicated affair. If a number of sources are being approached at the same time and deadlines are looming, it can be very difficult to keep everything organized. Adopt some type of simple bookkeeping system that helps keep track of actions taken or pending, upcoming grant deadlines, and any important information that has been learned about all funders. If the filmmaker has access to database software, then that can be an excellent tool for this task.

I prefer to have two different types of information readily available. One is a **Fundraising Journal**. This can be on paper, or on a computer file. Create a separate page for each and every funder. The page will have all contact information on it. After that, every time a contact is made with the foundation, it is entered in the journal chronologically. This is especially important to do right after having a conversation with any funder, so that information just learned can be placed in the journal. I turn to this journal before making a call to any funder, so that I can remind myself of what we talked about before. Here is a typical journal page:

THE GENEROUS CHARITABLE TRUST (GCT)
P.O. Box 75444
San Anselmo, CA 94732
Ph. 415.555.9335
Fax. 415.555.9336
www.gct.org
Contact: Astoria Buckes, Media Program Director
asbuckes@gct.org

Note: Astoria only available afternoons, Tu-Fri

2/16/08: Called about Project X. Astoria says "already heavily committed to film this year" — not hopeful about my chances, but she's heard of my work and wouldn't mind meeting for lunch.

2/26/08: Nice lunch date with Astoria at Le Burger Joint. Discovered she loves veggie burgers, enjoys jogging, raised in Missouri, ex-husband is 18th Century scholar. Foundation is pretty dry right now, doesn't see much chance for Project X. BUT, she did say if I ever get a number of other funders on board, and I'm short "just a bit" she might be able to kick in some discretionary funds at her disposal.

5/1/08: Called Astoria — reminded her of our lunch and told her I'd raised $190,000 and just need $10,000 more to complete the project. She requests full packet/proposal (sent) and says call in two weeks.

5/16/08: Call to Astoria — she's not ready yet. Call back again in 2 wks.

5/26/08: Yippee! Got the dough. Check to arrive in 2 wks. Astoria says "Be sure to give Foundation recognition in all publicity and in end credits." THANK YOU note sent right away to Foundation's Board of Trustees. Bought single orchid and hand delivered to Astoria.

6/5/08: Foundation check arrives.

10/5/08: E-Newsletter on Project X sent to AB.

1/1/09: Invite Astoria and Foundation staff to Project X premiere at Royale — she won't take comps and insists on buying 20 tix.

2/1/09: Final report sent to Foundation, along with DVD copy for their files.

6/1/09: Call to Astoria re funding new project, "Return of Project X" — she's receptive (Foundation loved the first film) and says send info then, "Let's have lunch."

Over a few years this journal becomes a very powerful tool for fundraising. Another list I recommend is a **Summary of Proposals** that provides a very quick visual representation of all proposal activity. This can be easily done on a spreadsheet, or in a journal. A typical format might be:

Date/ Amt. of Rqst.	Funder	Project	Results	Notes
5/1/09 $50,000	Ford Fndtn	Production	rjctd 7/01/03	
5/10/09 $10,000	Megabucks Fund	Scripting Phase	yes! on 6/30/03	
5/25/09 $100,000	ITVS	Completion Funds	(pending)	Call DL on 7/1

Keep this on a wall, a bulletin board, or separate computer document page so that it serves as an easy reminder of what proposals are still pending. For some positive reinforcement, try highlighting in yellow or circling in red any proposals that are accepted. The only other record-keeping device should be a set of separate manila folders devoted to storing information and correspondence with each funder over the years.

MORRIE'S MAXIMS

Before saying goodbye, I want to reiterate some points that have already been made, and bring up a few more. It is easy to feel overwhelmed by the enormous task of fundraising. And it is easy to lose sight of the bigger picture — how one film fits into the larger canvas of a whole career, and how fundraising is just one skill among many necessary to complete projects. So, just in case I have not been direct enough, let's revisit a few simple principles that help give context and focus to fundraising.

- ◆ **Personalize Everything**. Find ways to think like the funder, and provide the funder with the items that fulfill her needs. When possible, have communication come from someone already known to the funder.
- ◆ **Research Is Essential.** Research is just plain hard work, but must be done before approaching every and any funder.
- ◆ **Be Proactive.** Take control of every element in your environment that you can control, because even the smallest things are a reflection of your entire comportment.
- ◆ **Be Persistent.** Rejection is the norm in this business. Persistence pays off.
- ◆ **Write a Mission Statement.** Get clear about why filmmaking is absolutely essential to what you are trying to accomplish in the world, and be ready to articulate this mission to funders.
- ◆ **Learn How to Pitch.** Creating a brief and convincing pitch for each and every project is a baseline skill that must be part of the filmmaker's toolkit.
- ◆ **Network, Network, Network.** The best way to "curry serendipity" and increase the chances for unexpected positive

occurrences, is to get un-isolated and make as many contacts as possible. Make use of the new power of social networking to get connected.

- **Listen.** Learn the art of listening. Avoid monologue and invite dialogue as much as possible.
- **Say "Thank You."** Saying "thanks" costs almost nothing and reaps great rewards.
- **Stay in Touch.** Keep lines of communication open with past, present, and potential funders.
- **Market with Integrity.** Marketing is not a dirty word — it is an activity central to making a project and a filmmaker attractive to funders, and to helping a project ultimately find its audience. Find ways of marketing that are comfortable for you and your set of values.
- **Think Long-Term.** The journey of an independent filmmaker is a long one that takes stamina and a long-term vision. Think from A to Z, and not from A to B. Be willing to suffer many short-term losses in return for long-term gains.

I hope this book has empowered you to embark on the process of fundraising with vigor, enthusiasm, intelligence — and a high rate of success!. Please feel free to send along your fundraising stores, and any advice for additions or changes to future editions.

Now — go shake that money tree!

APPENDIX

SAMPLE GRANT #1 — ITVS

I am including the following proposal because it was successful in receiving support from The Independent Television Service (ITVS), which is one of the most important funders of independent work made for television. I know that many of you reading this book will be applying to ITVS. This proposal is by Judith Ehrlich and Rick Goldsmith and it is about Daniel Ellsberg, a central figure in the Watergate scandal that toppled Richard Nixon. This proposal follows the instructions from ITVS for what it wants. You will note that there is a heavy emphasis on the treatment — how the filmmakers plan to realize the story and what elements they will include. Ehrlich and Goldsmith do an excellent job of bringing the story alive. They have a lively and engaging opening paragraph. Their descriptions of who they want to reach and how they plan to reach them all sound plausible and well thought out. If you go to *www.mostdangerousman.org* you can view Ehrlich and Golsdsmith's three-minute fundraising clip. It's easy to see why the ITVS panel gave this project the greenlight for funding.

Judith Ehrlich; Rick Goldsmith - ITVS Phase 3 Application – PROGRAM DESCRIPTION

The Most Dangerous Man in America:
Daniel Ellsberg and the Pentagon Papers

SYNOPSIS

1971: America is embroiled in a dirty war based on lies. A president is abusing the power of his office, ignoring the will of the people, Congress and the courts. One man, at the center of power, armed with a safe full of secret documents, leaks the truth about the Vietnam War to the *New York Times*. He risks life in prison to stop the war he had helped to plan. His act of conscience and desperation triggers a Constitutional crisis, Watergate, and the only Presidential resignation in history and finally helps to end the war. Three decades later, he's still at it and the issues he unearthed — about secrecy, power and the people's right to know — are of more concern to America than ever.

TREATMENT

Format, Style, Structure and Approach

This documentary film is a three-act character-driven drama recounting real life events that reads like a John Le Carré novel. We intercut present-day interviews with the principal players of the Pentagon Papers story with innovative use of archival footage, and stretch artistically with use of re-creations animation and a driving, tension-filled soundtrack.

At the center of our story is the complex and charismatic Daniel Ellsberg. Bursting into national consciousness in June of 1971, the 40-year-old Ellsberg (in hours of archival footage) is intense, passionate and articulate — and a harsh critic of "imperial" presidency and governmental secrecy. Whether interviewed by Walter Cronkite while underground, surrounded by a crush of reporters, spending 90 minutes alone with Dick Cavett, or on trial for his life, the 1970s Ellsberg is as captivating as any politician or movie star, and his comments about America then resonate powerfully today. Our present-day interviews of the 76-year-old life-long activist reveal a man still intense, passionate and committed to his ideals, but also soul-searching, witty and reflective.

Ellsberg is joined on-screen by the principal players of the Pentagon Papers saga: Ellsberg's family, colleagues and critics; Pentagon Papers authors and government officials; Vietnam veterans, anti-war activists and Watergate principals; and the journalists who both covered the story and were an integral part of it. Our interviews are carefully lit by Director of Photography Vicente Franco, with a dark, ominous and ambiguous background, complementing their suspense-filled storytelling and incisive commentary.

What elevates our use of archival footage is that on the 1970s news and public affairs shows (as with the archival footage of Ellsberg), the issues and themes of our show are debated daily. Serious journalists offer us news analysis and commentary, on top of historical perspective. The network news reports of 1971, and again in early 1973 (with the Ellsberg trial), lead with the Ellsberg/Pentagon Papers story for weeks on end. News anchors like Walter Cronkite, John Chancellor and Howard K. Smith, and field reporters like Daniel Schorr, open a window on the transformation of the media itself.

Richard Nixon plays the role of antagonist to Ellsberg's protagonist. The daily (and incriminating) tapes made of his conversations in the Oval Office, gathered from the National "Abuse of Governmental Power" collection, reveal Nixon's obsession with, and personal vendetta against, Ellsberg. We also draw from more obscure sources, such as a stash of footage retrieved from the dumpster behind the Los Angeles CBS affiliate, and the Ellsbergs' complete and extensive family photo collection, which bring the film a poignant intimacy.

The filmic quality of this documentary will be heightened by using tasteful and sparing animated sequences, re-creations and special effects. They will illustrate two major themes in the film: secrets — keeping them and revealing them — and the power of words and documents. The mood will be defined by an evocative soundscape appropriate to a political thriller. We will layer recorded and archival audio with a minimalist musical score evoking danger, risk, fear and possibility.

Title Sequence in hand-drawn animation
(in the style of *Eyes on the Prize*)
A figure opens a safe and fills a briefcase with papers stamped
"TOP SECRET." He walks past the guard and out the door marked
"Rand Corporation." The soundtrack is ominous, tense and built on
the rhythm of a 1969 Xerox machine. It is dark, only the intermit-
tent green light of the copier illuminates the room.

We zoom in to see the words "TOP SECRET" as they are cut from
a page and spirited away. In quick succession come the phrases
"communist military threat," "classified U.S. intelligence," "need
to increase U.S. combat troops." The words drift out the window,
through a door with the *New York Times* masthead, and attach
themselves to the newsprint. Loudly, the newsprint presses roll. Out
flows the headline "Pentagon Study Traces 3 Decades of Growing
U.S. Involvement" as in *voice over and then on camera,* a young
Daniel Ellsberg at a podium intones, "I did this because I felt the
concealment of this information for 25 years led to the death of
50,000 Americans and several hundred thousand Vietnamese..."

Ellsberg continues, voice under, as another figure appears, Egil
"Bud" Krogh, former Nixon White House aide: "We felt we were
dealing with a national security crisis. Henry Kissinger said Daniel
Ellsberg was 'the most dangerous man in America' and he *had to be
stopped*!"

> *Music swell.*
> **Title: The Most Dangerous Man in America: Daniel Ellsberg
> and the Pentagon Papers**
> *Fade out.*

Act 1: The Cold Warrior — an interior, personal story of tragedy
and ambition, and of spiritual and political transformation.

*Boston, 1959. The ivy-covered walls of Harvard University. Still of
a young, self-assured, ex-Marine Dan Ellsberg.* Professor Richard
Falk recalls: "Dan was perhaps *the* leading young war planner in
America, a cold warrior to the core." Ellsberg guest-lectures at
Harvard for Dr. Henry Kissinger. Ellsberg and Kissinger begin a
collegial relationship that will last a dozen years before it ruptures

dramatically. *Stills of Ellsberg with other Pentagon personnel.* Ellsberg moves easily among the hawks, becomes a Pentagon insider and advisor to President Kennedy. He thrives on seeing "patterns" and devising clever military strategy. At the same time he is intensely wary and even alarmist about the possibility of nuclear war.

A 1940s car travels, skids, twists, and there is an obscene CRASH. Dan, seated at the piano, recounts the story of his father, driving his family, then falling asleep at the wheel. The crash killed Dan's mother and sister and put 15-year-old Dan in the hospital. Dan: "I've often thought that maybe the significance of this accident is that I, more than my peers, can imagine catastrophe. To others, nuclear catastrophe is remote, to me, it is real. It is always real, and the worst is always possible, even probable."

Ellsberg's hands play the classical etude, lyrically. The camera PANS from hands on piano keyboard to the large framed portrait of a beautiful woman — his wife of 35 years, Patricia Marx Ellsberg. "I met him at a party," recalls the toy company heiress. "'Stay away from him,' I was told. 'He's brilliant, but dangerous.'" Like a moth to a flame, the anti-war public radio reporter is drawn to the war strategist. "'How can you be dating a war-monger?' asked my pacifist friends." But the two, hawk and dove, do indeed fall in love. And then Ellsberg, the former Marine, tests their bond when he abruptly volunteers to go to Vietnam on a fact-finding mission for the Pentagon.

Vietnam, 1965: Stills of Ellsberg, jauntily displaying his AK-47 hung from his shoulder, and in the high grass with a rifle. Firefights, chaos, explosions, snipers. Patricia and Dan recount her visiting him in Vietnam, and both acknowledge — Dan with a smile, Patricia a frown — that he was turned on by the adrenaline rush of risk and danger, and that they suffered a seemingly irreparable break because of their differences over the war.

But Dan, too, is drawn to the Vietnamese villagers, the children, and severely disturbed by the horror America (and he) have wrought upon the populace. Dan remembers coming upon a burning village, the children scraping to find some lost dolls. "That scene was extremely anguishing for me — this is what the war meant to them, the destruction of their homes. And their lives." He now sees the war as both unwinnable and morally indefensible, and begins to question the "American" perspective.

A sterile three-story building in Santa Monica, California. Journalist Ben Bagdikian recalls, "There was more IQ per square foot at the Rand Corporation than anywhere in America." Many of Rand's "best and brightest" are recruited to do a detailed study of the history of the Vietnam War, ordered by Defense Secretary Robert McNamara. Mort Halperin, staff chief of the study: "It was top-secret, as everyone knows, but not to keep it from the Russians or the Viet Cong, but to keep it from President Johnson. McNamara feared if LBJ knew about the study, he would shut us down."

Ellsberg works on the study, reads the study. *Words, phrases jump off the pages, swirl around Ellsberg. Secrets, startling revelations.* Ellsberg has discovered: four Presidents, Truman through Johnson, have known the war was unwinnable, and all escalated nonetheless. Then they all lied to the American people.

Archival montage of events: A crushing defeat for American during Tet, 1968. LBJ "shall not seek, nor will I accept" his party's nomination. Richard Nixon, with a "secret plan" to end the war, wins the Presidency, and he brings a familiar figure on board as National Security Advisor: Henry Kissinger, Ellsberg recalls a December 1968 meeting with Kissinger, who sought out Ellsberg for advice on Vietnam. Ellsberg urges Kissinger to read the massive McNamara study on Vietnam. Kissinger told me, 'I wouldn't learn much from it.' I learned soon that Kissinger and Nixon had their own plans."

"Dan pumped me for information, he was obsessed," says Mort Halperin, Kissinger's aide in 1969. From Halperin, Ellsberg learns about yet more escalation in Southeast Asia, and plans to use nuclear weapons. Horrified at Nixon's war expansion, into Cambodia, into Laos, Ellsberg finally begins to speak out.

We take the bumpy ride away from the centers of power with Dan Ellsberg. Again he is inspired by text, reading Thoreau and Gandhi, and by the example of Randy Kehler, principled draft resister who chooses prison over service in an unjust war. Ellsberg describes watching Kehler go to jail for his beliefs, then finding himself sobbing uncontrollably on the men's room floor. "'What can I do to stop this war,' I asked myself." The answer, he finally realizes, lies in the 7,000-page McNamara report that lives in his Rand Corporation safe.

A re-creation: The briefcase is carried past the unsuspecting night watchman. The eerie green light of the Xerox machine blinks on and off. "Top Secret" is snipped off page after page. Act 1 ends as Ellsberg — with his colleague Anthony Russo, and curiously, his 13-year-old son Robert — begins the long process of Xeroxing 7,000 pages, one by one, night after night.

Act 2: The Leak Heard 'Round the World — The story now becomes a public story of headlines and international breaking news, shifts in public consciousness and challenges to the power relationships that govern our nation.

"It was the Everest of leaks," remembers Hedrick Smith of the *New York Times.* "We couldn't believe our eyes — cables from Presidents to Generals, from Kennedy to Lodge, from Johnson to Westmoreland. We always knew we'd been lied to — now we had the proof."

The reporters are gung-ho, but, recounts James Goodale, the *Times'* legal counsel, "It was a risk of an institution. We had to answer — and answer correctly — the most basic question: 'Do we have a right to publish classified documents?'" Lawyers, publisher and editors struggle with the question: to publish or not to publish? Washington bureau chief Max Frankel: "If we backed down, we wouldn't have been able to look each other in the eye."

The newspapers speed through the presses, then hit the streets. It is June 13, 1971. The New York Times publishes—the first of a series of articles on "a secret archives of the Vietnam War." We follow the story through the Network News reports, new revelations and breaking news every day.

At once, across the nation, an explosion of news, questions, and Constitutional confrontations. Did Johnson lie to win the election over Goldwater in '64? Was Kennedy behind the assassination of Diem in '63? Is the *Times* publication legal? Responsible? Treasonous? Does the public have a right to know what have been up till now government secrets, even classified documents?

Spindles, capstans and reels turn rhythmically on a tape recorder. On the secret Nixon tapes: "It's treasonous," says Henry Kissinger. "If whole file cabinets can disappear you can't have orderly government anymore." *Back-and-forth phone calls* between Nixon, Kissinger, top aides and Attorney General John Mitchell. *On Day 4 of the stories, headline in the* New York Times: *"Pentagon Papers Stories Stopped by Nixon Administration Injunction"*. It is a Constitutional confrontation that will go all the way to the Supreme Court within two weeks. The ramifications will be felt by the media and the country for decades to come.

Ben Bagdikian at the *Washington Post* remembers, "I got a call — he didn't identify himself, but I knew it was Dan. He said, 'I have something you'll want. If I give it to you will you publish it?'" And so the *Post* publishes the Pentagon Papers and then they too are slapped with an injunction. Movement friend and history professor Howard Zinn recalls Dan, pursued now by the FBI, going into hiding, and helping him get copies of the Pentagon Papers to 17 other newspapers, who continue to publish. "They couldn't stop them, it was like herding bees," says Ellsberg.

"CBS Evening News: A Special Report: A Conversation with Daniel Ellsberg". Still underground, Ellsberg was filmed with Walter Cronkite at a secret location. "Should the President be making foreign policy without the help of the Congress, the press, the people?" Ellsberg says to Cronkite and the nation. "Perhaps we've been playing follow the leader too long,"

Boston. Outside the federal courthouse, amidst a crush of reporters, Ellsberg has turned himself in, two weeks after the first Times *story.* Ellsberg is asked if he's afraid of going to jail. Defiant, indignant: "Wouldn't you risk going to prison to help end this war?"

A traitor to some, the indicted Ellsberg emerges an instant celebrity. *The Dick Cavett Show.* Ellsberg receives a one-minute ovation when introduced. He seems born to the spotlight it, relishes it, and makes good use of his bully pulpit:

> "We have not demanded enough in the way of respon-
> sibility from our public servants. Tell them, 'It is not
> acceptable to us for you to make choices that lead to
> these deaths of our sons and Vietnamese sons. It is not
> acceptable to say, In order to be re-elected I must keep
> my mouth shut when I know important crimes and
> truths are being concealed.'"

Ellsberg has become a hero to millions. But not to all.

"He was one of my closest friends," says Harry Rowen, director of the Rand Institute. "I trusted him. His security breech put the entire institute at risk." Was Ellsberg's leak a betrayal? Morton Halperin, "I sympathized with his passion for ending the war," says Mort Halperin. "But I felt betrayed, too, and to this day, I can't say he did the right thing." Dan bristles at this. "Betraying a company and even friends vs. staying silent in the face of government lying and a murderous, unjust war? I wish more people would choose the first."

Dark music. An archival montage of events: Richard Nixon car-ries on the Vietnam War as if the Pentagon Papers never happened. The anti-war movement dissipates. Despite an emerging Watergate scandal, President Nixon wins re-election in 1972 in the biggest landslide in American history. He resumes the bombing of North Vietnam, the mining of Haiphong Harbor. Will the Pentagon Papers become just a small historical footnote after all?

Act 3: President Nixon vs. Daniel Ellsberg

January, 1973, Los Angeles. The trial of Daniel Ellsberg and his "co-conspirator" Anthony Russo opens. Defense attorney Len Weinglass: "The judge asks the jury pool, 'how many of you have heard of or read the Pentagon Papers?' Out of 90 people, only two of them raised their hands. Dan leans over the defense table and whispers to the rest of us, 'For this, I risked 115 years in prison?'"

The evening news intercut with reflections from Ellsberg, Weinglass, Russo, Falk, Zinn: It all starts badly. There is jealousy and friction between the Russo and Ellsberg camps. Ellsberg takes the stand in his own defense and is visibly shaken. Judge Matthew Byrne rules against the defense — who want to introduce the criminality of the Vietnam War — time after time.

And then, abruptly, John Chancellor on NBC News: "At the Pentagon Papers trial in California today, it was revealed that E. Howard Hunt, convicted in the Watergate conspiracy, planned the burglary of Daniel Ellsberg's psychiatrist, in a meeting at the White House." A barrage of news reports follows, incriminating the Nixon Administration and his creation of a "Plumbers" unit ("we stop leaks"), with the express purpose of discrediting Daniel Ellsberg in the media.

Suddenly, it is no longer Daniel Ellsberg on trial, but Richard Nixon. The Nixon White House tapes reveal the President, on tape, plotting the dirty tricks against Ellsberg. *Nixon on tape: "I know how to play this game and I play it gloves off!"* White House figures John Dean and "Plumbers" head Egil Krogh, on-camera today, pull the curtain back further on the workings of the Nixon White House.

More twists, turns and revelations every day: illegal secret wiretaps on Ellsberg, Nixon offers trial judge Byrne the directorship of the FBI. As the trial reaches its climax, Ellsberg holds court among a throng of reporters, delivering a riveting civics lesson: how those in power use secrecy and dirty tricks to bypass democracy; the lengths they will go to stifle dissent; and how President Nixon deserves *his* day in court to defend his transgressions.

Headline: Ellsberg Case Dismissed. Judge Byrne declares a mistrial and Ellsberg is free. Ellsberg has set an example of citizen action, taken to the limit, and has emerged vindicated. Richard Nixon resigns a year later, waving goodbye to America on the tarmac, his Vietnam policy finally in tatters, America's forces pulled out of Vietnam, the violence there finally ebbing. The emperor has been exposed, due in no small part, through a wild and twisting road, by events that began with the Pentagon Papers.

Epilogue
Dan Ellsberg endures. He continues his fight for an open democracy, an end to war, an end to the Imperial Presidency. And he

continues that fight today. He's had 80 arrests on behalf of big war-and-peace issues. He is the "go-to" guy for other whistle-blowers, around the world. His presence and his never-ending activism challenge Americans to ever question the pronouncements of their leaders, to become active, to speak truth to power, and to take seriously the phrase "we the people."

Program length: Our original proposal to ITVS was written for a PBS hour-long program. In developing the project further, we are convinced the correct length for this film is 90 minutes. This treatment reflects the complexity of the story as history and psychological study of a unique character in American history. We feel strongly now we can only do the story justice in this longer format. Ellsberg Attorney Lenny Weinglass told us, you could teach an entire course in law school on this legal case. Complete courses are taught in more than one American Studies program on the Pentagon Papers. This is a complex and dramatic story that will easily entertain and enlighten the PBS audience for 90 minutes.

Reason the program is appropriate for public television: This film fulfils a stated mission of PBS. Its "dedication to spreading awareness, unlocking mysteries and exposing truths." We had very enthusiastic meetings with Yance Ford of POV and Kathryn Lo of PBS at the IFP Market (letters to follow). Public television in Europe is also very interested in this story. John Battsek of Passion Pictures, London has approached us to Executive Produce our film. Battsek met with Richard Klein at BBC and Nick Frazer at Storyville last week where there is definite interest. Hans Robert Eisenhauer of ZDF/Arte stated similar interest in our meeting at the IFP Market.

Target Audience: Younger viewers for whom this is an unknown and potentially empowering story would particularly benefit from this program. Those under 40 have no recall of this historic act of civic courage that shook American society. In a time of media complacency in the face of a questionable war and a President ignoring the Constitutional bounds of his office, this is a story that empowers those encountering such misuse of governmental power for the first time. As a teacher at community college, a former high school teacher and a former curriculum developer for this age group, Ehrlich is experienced in reaching youth. Both filmmakers are parents of teenagers. This story would also appeal to groups who are being targeted for wiretapping, suspicion and restriction of free speech, i.e. Muslims, Arabs and South Asian Americans. At the moment this film tells a story vital to all American voters, citizen and non-citizen participants in the political process, those concerned with questions of the misuse of government power and secrecy system. This film will be a guidepost to concerned citizens looking for historical precedents of civil courage in times of failed leadership and "Imperial Presidency." This film will definitely appeal to people over 50 who remember the name Daniel Ellsberg and the Pentagon Papers, but have forgotten what he did, why and probably never knew the depth and breadth of his act and the consequences but would like to know. On the Web this film will provide in-depth resources for citizens and government insiders inspired to become active.

Project status: Our distribution plan will be ambitious. At this moment we have possibilities of theatrical distribution domestically and internationally as well as European broadcast. POV and PBS have stated interest in this program for the PBS audience. Kathryn Lo has offered to present it to *American Experience*. All three major international distributors, Annie Rooney, WGBH International and Films Transit are interested in working with us to reach the international TV market.

With Peter Broderick's advice and ongoing consultation we are prepared to identify and create partnerships with the dozens of nonprofit organizations concerned with issues of free speech, free press, civil liberties, open society, open government, opposition to the secrecy system, peace, opposition to wire-tapping, the rights of whistle blowers and the limits of executive power. Daniel Ellsberg also raises questions of ethical behavior in the face of war and acting on the basis of conscience that has resonance for the faith-based and ethics communities. We plan to identify and reach a targeted audience for DVD sales and substantive educational outreach. We look forward to working with ITVS staff to develop an expansive and useful Web site and targeted outreach campaign as they did for "The Good War and Those Who Refused to Fight It".

	A	B	C	D	E	F	G	H	I
1	TOTAL PRODUCTION BUDGET								
2	PROGRAM NAME: The Most Dangerous Man in America								
3									
4	100-Producing Staff	# of UNITS	UNIT DESCRIPTION (i.e. flat, hour, day, week)	COST per UNIT	sub-total	SPENT TO DATE (as of 7/22/08)	ESTIMATE TO COMPLETE	PAID FOR BY ITVS	TOTAL (# of UNITS x Cost per Unit)
5	100-Producer/Director (Ehrlich)*	17	months	7,500		53,883	73,617	62,000	127,500
6	101-Producer/Director/Editor (Goldsmith)	17	months	7,500		53,500	74,000	62,000	127,500
7	102-Associate Producer*	11	months	4,200		5,250	40,950	31,801	46,200
8	103-Assistant Producer	11	months	1,500		2,137	14,363	11,085	16,500
9	104-Bookeeping-accounting	10	months	150		175	1,325	1,000	1,500
10	105-administrative assts/clerical		allow			259	1,141	800	1,400
11	TOTAL Producing Staff					115,204	205,396	168,686	320,600
12									
13	300-Travel	# of UNITS	UNIT DESCRIPTION (i.e. flat, hour, day, week)	COST per UNIT	sub-total	SPENT TO DATE (as of 7/22/08)	ESTIMATE TO COMPLETE	PAID FOR BY ITVS	TOTAL (# of UNITS x Cost per Unit)
14	301-Ground and Air travel		allow			6,965	3,535	3,200	10,500
15	302-Per Diem/meals		allow			3,524	1,976	1,500	5,500
16	303-Hotel		allow			741	759	500	1,500
17	TOTAL Travel					11,230	6,270	5,200	17,500
18									
19	400- Production expense	# of UNITS	UNIT DESCRIPTION (i.e. flat, hour, day, week)	COST per UNIT	sub-total	SPENT TO DATE (as of 7/22/08)	ESTIMATE TO COMPLETE	PAID FOR BY ITVS	TOTAL (# of UNITS x Cost per Unit)
20	Production supplies- media (itemized below)					x	x		x
21	DVCam Tape Stock	90	tapes	20	1,800	x	x		x
22	MiniDV Tapes (for safety clones)	90	tapes	3	270	x	x		x
23	miniDV tape stock (for archival footage	60	tapes	3	180	x	x		x
24	blank dvds and cases	200	dvds & cases	2	400	x	x		x
25	Master tapes and stock		allow		1,000	x	x		x
26	401-Production supplies- media TOTAL					2,328	1,322	1,322	3,650
27	402-Archival- screeners, photos, supplies		allow			929	2,071	2,071	3,000
28	403-R&D supplies and costs		allow			614	386	386	1,000
29	404-Print materials		allow			1,555	945		2,500
30	405-Prodn/post-prodn misc. supplies		allow				500		500
31	TOTAL Production expense					5,426	5,224	3,779	10,650
32									

	A	B	C	D	E	F	G	H	I
33									
34	500-Production crew and equipment rental	# of UNITS	UNIT DESCRIPTION (i.e. flat, hour, day, week)	COST per UNIT	sub-total	SPENT TO DATE (as of 7/22/08)	ESTIMATE TO COMPLETE	PAID FOR BY ITVS	TOTAL (# of UNITS x Cost per Unit)
35	501-Director of Photography (Franco)	25	days	750		11,043	7,707	6,000	18,750
36	502-Sound Recordist	20	days	450		3,350	5,650	3,600	9,000
37	503-Production Manager	0	days	300			-		-
38	504-Camera rental	22	days	400		5,120	3,680	2,800	8,800
39	505-Sound equipment rental	14	days	50		300	400	400	700
40	506-Production crew-other (gaffer, PA)		allow			530	470		1,000
41	TOTAL Production crew and equipment rental					20,343	17,907	12,800	38,250
42									
43	600-Consultation	# of UNITS	UNIT DESCRIPTION (i.e. flat, hour, day, week)	COST per UNIT	sub-total	SPENT TO DATE (as of 7/22/08)	ESTIMATE TO COMPLETE	PAID FOR BY ITVS	TOTAL (# of UNITS x Cost per Unit)
44	601-Consultants-prodn & distribution		allow			2,592	208		2,800
45	602-Consultants-academic advisors	4	consultants	250			1,000		1,000
46	TOTAL					2,592	1,208	-	3,800
47									
48	700-Post-production	# of UNITS	UNIT DESCRIPTION (i.e. flat, hour, day, week)	COST per UNIT	sub-total	SPENT TO DATE (as of 7/22/08)	ESTIMATE TO COMPLETE	PAID FOR BY ITVS	TOTAL (# of UNITS x Cost per Unit)
49	701-Editor (Goldsmith)	49	weeks	-			-		-
50	702-Archival research	25	days	150		2,650	1,100	1,100	3,750
51	703-Transcriber	45	tapes	100		2,679	1,821	1,821	4,500
52	704-Edit equip rental (from prod'rs)		allow			2,500	4,500	2,000	7,000
53	705-Post-prodn expenses- drives, etc.					4,772	1,428	1,428	6,200
54	705-Assistant Editor*	49	weeks	1,000		9,400	39,600	36,000	49,000
55	707-Composer		flat				15,000	5,000	15,000
56	708-Music recording		allow				1,500		1,500
57	709-Sound Design & Edit + Pro Tools	4	weeks	3,000			12,000	5,000	12,000
58	710-Animation		fee				13,000	5,000	13,000
59	711-Graphic Design		allow				3,000	2,000	3,000
60	712-Tape-to-tape on-line studio & editor with color correction	9	days	2,500			22,500	14,000	22,500
61	713-Audio studio & sound mix, incl. editor	32	hours	425			13,600	8,000	13,600
62	714-Consulting editor	75	hours	100		-	7,500	2,500	7,500
63	715-Closed Captioning	1.5	hours	1,000			1,500	1,500	1,500
64	716-Publicity Stills (black & white)		allow				2,500	2,500	2,500
65	717-Transcription for ITVS Cuts		allow				900	900	900
66	718-Narrator		allow					800	800
67	719-Narration recording	4	hours	125			500		500
68	720-Music Cue Sheet Prep.		allow				300	300	300
69	721-Edit room rental, off-line	28	months	324		5,832	3,240	3,240	9,072
70	TOTAL					27,833	144,989	93,589	174,122
71									

	A	B	C	D	E	F	G	H	I
72									
73									
74	**800-Archival, rights and license fees**	# of UNITS	UNIT DESCRIPTION (i.e. flat, hour, day, week)	COST per UNIT	sub-total	SPENT TO DATE (as of 7/22/08)	ESTIMATE TO COMPLETE	PAID FOR BY ITVS	TOTAL (# of UNITS x Cost per Unit)
75	801-Story rights		contract			5,000	15,000	5,000	20,000
76	802-Footage Rights	450	seconds	75.00			33,750	30,000	33,750
77	803-Archival tapes- dup for src masters		allow				3,000	1,000	3,000
78	804-Music license Fees	2	pieces	1,500			3,000	1,500	3,000
79	805-Still photo Rights		allow				2,500	1,500	2,500
80	**TOTAL**					5,000	57,250	39,000	62,250
81									
82	**900-Office, Administration and Insurance**	# of UNITS	UNIT DESCRIPTION (i.e. flat, hour, day, week)	COST per UNIT	sub-total	SPENT TO DATE (as of 7/22/08)	ESTIMATE TO COMPLETE	PAID FOR BY ITVS	TOTAL (# of UNITS x Cost per Unit)
83	901-Office supplies/copying/printing		allow			1,614	786	700	2,400
84	902-Postage and shipping		allow			1,223	577	577	1,800
85	903-Telephone and internet	12	months	180		320	1,840	1,840	2,160
86	904-General Liability and equipment Insurance					2,940			2,940
87	905-Worker's Compensation						1,897	500	1,897
88	906-Errors & Omissions Insurance						4,000	4,000	4,000
89	907-Grant management fee		allow			3,532	3,968		7,500
90	908-Legal costs		allow				5,000		5,000
91	909-Production office rent	10	months	960			9,600	8,000	9,600
92	910-web site design and maintenance		allow				2,080	1,000	2,080
93	910-Bank and merchant services fees		allow			71	329	329	400
94	Payroll expenses (FICA, SUI)					5,042	13,041	12,000	18,083
95	**TOTAL**					14,742	43,118	28,946	57,860
96									
97									
98									
99	**PRODUCTION BUDGET**					SPENT TO DATE (as of 7/22/08)	ESTIMATE TO COMPLETE	PAID FOR BY ITVS	TOTAL
100	100-Producing Staff					115,204	205,396	168,686	320,600
101	300-Travel					11,230	6,270	5,200	17,500
102	400- Production expense					5,426	5,224	3,779	10,650
103	500-Production crew and equipment rental					20,343	17,907	12,800	38,250
104	600-Consultation					2,592	1,208	-	3,800
105	700-Post-production					27,833	144,989	93,589	174,122
106	800-Archival, rights and license fees					5,000	57,250	39,000	62,250
107	900-Office, Administration and Insurance					14,742	43,118	28,946	57,860
108	**TOTAL budget**					202,370	481,362	352,000	685,032

SAMPLE GRANT #2 —
BEHIND THE VELVET CURTAIN

This proposal is a great example of what you would send a foundation or a government funder. It is well written, compelling, and the visual presentation is extremely attractive (though it could use contact information for the filmmakers right up front and not just at the end). As of publication date, the project has raised money from the California Council for the Humanities, the Lucius and Eva Eastman Fund, the Small Change Foundation, individual donors, and immediate friends and family.

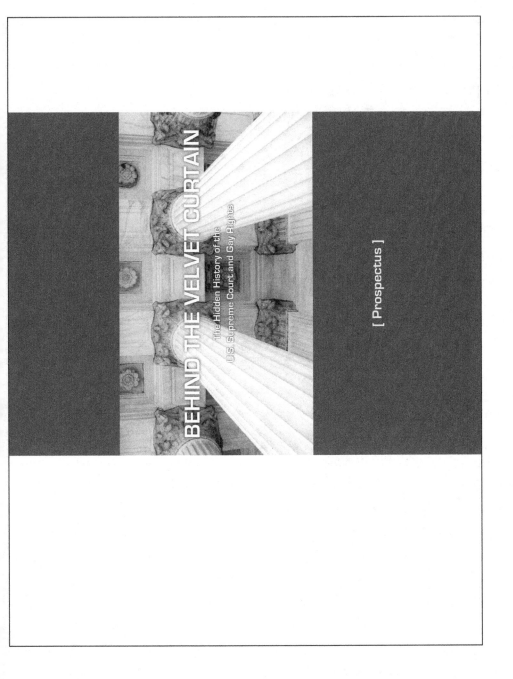

BEHIND THE VELVET CURTAIN

The Hidden History of the
U.S. Supreme Court and Gay Rights

[Prospectus]

BEHIND THE VELVET CURTAIN

The Hidden History of the U.S. Supreme Court and Gay Rights

[Prospectus]

Introduction / Background 1
Narrative Summary, Structure and Aesthetics 3
Point of View 7
Audience, Distribution and Digital Media Strategies 9
Budget and Fundraising Plan 13
The Filmmakers 15

Appendix A: The Story 19
Appendix B: Interview Subjects 27
Appendix C: Project Advisors 29
Appendix D: Comprehensive Budget 31

© 2008 Aquarius Media

Introduction / Background

"I'm not sure the world is ready for this . . ."

"Taking this case would be a disaster . . . The heat of the
Moral Majority would fall upon the Court . . . Let the matter die."

— Supreme Court confidential memoranda about gay rights cases

Behind the Velvet Curtain uses a traditional feature-length documentary and companion digital media audience engagement program to chronicle a story that begins in the early 1950s and continues in the present day: a dramatic account of how the highest court in the land has struggled with the hot-button issue of human rights for gays and lesbians. The investigation looks behind the scenes at the Supreme Court to reveal the remarkable journeys taken by a handful of justices: What does it take to change the minds and reach the hearts of a court? Of a society?

Every major social and political issue is brought to the Supreme Court and the decisions made by its nine justices have real and lasting impacts. At a time when the Court is deciding Presidential elections, defining what it means to torture and arguing about which methods of execution are 'cruel or unusual,' the institution remains prominent and influential not just domestically but worldwide. Particularly in the realm of civil and human rights, the Court's power is unequal-

In the early 1950s the F.B.I. and the Postal Service try to silence the fledgling gay movement, calling the mere acknowledgment of homosexuality 'obscene.'

led; beginning with the desegregation cases of the 1950s and continuing with rulings to advance women's rights, religious freedoms and protections for the disabled, this institution has been a cornerstone of the United States' moral authority on the global stage.

Yet the inner workings of this tribunal remain largely hidden from the public. What do we really know about how the Supreme Court approaches its most controversial questions? If we could peer behind the Court's velvet curtain – at the secret struggles and debates, the strategizing and maneuvering, the unseen prejudices and compromises – would we feel more or less confidence in this institution? Would our understanding of the Court's influence on American society be altered? How might future civil and human rights struggles be shaped by a deeper knowledge of the Court?

One of the most fascinating and revealing aspects of the Court's hidden history is its inconsistent and sometimes anguished attempts to address gay and lesbian rights. Amid many controversial and politically charged issues, gay rights stands out, according to insiders, as the one area the Court worked to avoid for decades. Despite this seeming indifference, gay men and women for more than 50 years have been turning to the Court hoping for fair hearings. In fact, the Supreme Court has heavily influenced the course of gay rights since the 1950s. In more than 80 gay rights cases – those heard as well as those turned away – the Court has had a profound impact not just on individual lives, but on the civil and human rights of millions.

Because the Supreme Court operates in virtual secrecy, little is public about the way justice is weighed and decisions are made. While even the President is subject to the public accountability requirements of the Freedom of Information Act, the Court has avoided scrutiny by deliberating in complete isolation and classifying its papers as the personal property of individual justices, who are free to seal, purge or destroy these records. Despite this secrecy, thorough investigation has uncovered substantial and surprising facts about the Court's gay rights history. Handwritten notes made by the justices, confidential memos made public for the first time, as well as interviews with former clerks, colleagues, family members and observers reveal the messy truth about the Court's struggle to comprehend homosexuality and come to terms with demands for gay and lesbian equality.

Handwritten notes made by the justices, confidential memos made public for the first time, as well as interviews with former clerks, colleagues and family members reveal the messy truth about the Court's struggle with gay rights.

The behind-the-scenes account of how the Supreme Court has handled gay rights is part tragedy, part triumph.

Full of cliffhanger moments and reversals of fortune, these are the David-and-Goliath stories of everyday men and women who braved both physical danger and contempt to stand up for their most basic freedoms. Much more than a series of courtroom dramas, however, *Behind the Velvet Curtain* is the chronicle of a 50-year journey taken by the Court and the society it reflects and governs. What does it take for people to change their minds? What does it take for the high court, and a majority of Americans, to accept and ultimately welcome a hidden and despised minority as full citizens with equal rights and liberties? If the principles of fairness and equality are core American values, the high court's journey beyond anti-gay prejudice and bigotry is one of the defining legal, ethical and moral chapters of American history.

Narrative Summary

"Very few people who are in great positions of power go through real interior change . . ."
—Journalist Jack Newfield

Although the subject matter is serious and its history rich with detail, the fight for gay rights in America's highest court is gripping, entertaining and ultimately moving. The stories of men and women who turn to the Court for justice propel the plot and illustrate what is at stake. Yet it is behind the scenes at the Court where we come to understand the unique forces at play in decisions that carry such vivid, real-life consequences for the people involved.

The cast of characters includes J. Edgar Hoover, Anita Bryant, the Boy Scouts and the I.N.S., as well as everyday people who stand up for their rights before one of the most powerful and shrouded courts in the world. This is the story of men in an L.A. bar who kiss at the stroke of midnight, New Year's Eve, are arrested by undercover cops and forced to register as sex offenders... The story of a Minnesota woman fighting for the right to see and care for her partner, institutionalized by a drunk driver... The story of a New York family ripped apart when the government steps up deportation of homosexual "psychopaths"... The story of a Seattle man accused of "flaunting" his homosexuality

A Santa Monica restaurateur makes his feelings known, circa 1964. 'Anybody does any recruiting, I say shoot him. Who cares?'

and fired – from a job at the Equal Employment Opportunity Commission.

As moving as these human dramas are, the most compelling characters in *Behind the Velvet Curtain* turn out to be the Supreme Court justices and staff whose personal journeys are profiled. This is the story of the justice who caves to secret pressure from a colleague to switch his vote at the 11th hour, handing the gay community its worst defeat... The story of the justice who grows close to his lesbian neighbors and who in the 1960s emerges as the gay community's first passionate defender behind the velvet curtain... The story of the closeted clerk who agonizes over whether to come out to his boss, and who becomes a

133

pariah in the gay community after his boss casts the deciding anti-gay vote in a key case... The story of the justice who begins his career ruling against gay litigants and ends up penning the high court's most passionate plea for the right to love and be let alone.

The most fascinating and important theme the film explores is that of people who change their minds: nine men and women in positions of extreme power, some of whom evolve to believe the principles of fairness and equality should supersede their own private prejudices. The movement toward full equality for homosexuals is a revolution that American society has been undergoing for more than 50 years, and which is embodied by the personal journeys of a handful of justices. It is these justices who confront their own biases and, often to their own astonishment, lead the charge within the Court for fair treatment of gays and lesbians. It is these justices who are the unlikely heroes of our story.

The film has natural divisions into three parts, each corresponding to a discrete period of American social and political history, LGBT history and Court history. Each act explores the personal evolution of a single justice.

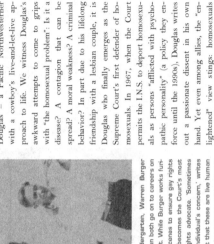

Friends since kindergarten, Warren Burger and Harry Blackmun both go on to careers on the Supreme Court. While Burger works furiously behind the scenes to ensure gay rights losses, Blackmun becomes the Court's most passionate gay rights advocate. Sometimes we overlook the individual's concern,' writes Blackmun, 'the fact that these are live human beings that are so deeply and terribly affected by our decisions.'

Act I ("1953 – 1969: Faggots Stay Out") is about the emergence of a visible homosexual minority and society's attempts to keep that minority silent. The central character of this act is maverick Justice William Douglas – a Pacific Northwesterner with a cowboy's live-and-let-live approach to life. We witness Douglas's awkward attempts to come to grips with "the homosexual problem": Is it a disease? A contagion that can be spread? A moral weakness? A criminal behavior? In part due to his lifelong friendship with a lesbian couple, it is Douglas who finally emerges as the Supreme Court's first defender of homosexuals. In 1967, when the Court permits the I.N.S. to deport homosexuals as persons "afflicted with psychopathic personality" (a policy they enforce until the 1990s), Douglas writes out a passionate dissent in his own hand. Yet even among allies, the "enlightened" view stings: homosexuals deserve not condemnation, but pity.

Act II ("1969 – 1986: Flaunting It") sees the closet doors kicked down. No longer on the defensive, gays push for basic freedoms. A society – and a Court – that spent decades trying to silence the homosexual voice and smother the nascent homosexual movement is now faced with activists demanding equality. Justice Harry Blackmun, appointed by Nixon to pull the Court rightward, becomes the unlikely hero of this act. By 1986, when the Court delivers a devastating blow in its *Bowers v. Hardwick* decision (upholding the arrest of a Georgia man for having consensual sex with another adult male in the privacy of his bedroom) it is Blackmun – a man who 15 years earlier viewed being openly gay as justification for losing one's job – who pens a moving dissent and reads it from the bench to underscore the case's significance. Later Blackmun confides how agonized he has been: he still believes homosexuality is immoral, but he believes even more in "the right to be let alone."

In Act III ("1986 – 2008: A Place At The Table") efforts to exclude homosexuals from American society are stepped up. The country, forced to acknowledge the existence of homosexuals, is saying, "We don't have to accept you as equals". St. Patrick's Day parade organizers refuse to march with Irish homosexuals. Boy Scout troupes purge known gay people from their ranks. The U.S. Olympic Committee blocks homosexuals from staging a "Gay Olympics" (while ignoring the Armenian Olympics, Crab Cooking Olympics and even Rat Olympics). But in the 90s the tide turns. The Court begins to discern the animus fueling attacks on gays. It is another conservative justice, Reagan appointee Anthony Kennedy, who emerges in this act as the surprise champion of gay rights. Despite a record of anti-gay rulings

Justice Lewis Powell in 1986 caves to secret lobbying and changes his vote on *Bowers v. Hardwick,* handing the gay movement its biggest high court defeat. He later says, "I probably made a mistake."

early in his career, Kennedy stuns observers in 2003 by spearheading the gay community's biggest legal win: *Lawrence v. Texas.* Journalist Jan Crawford Greenburg describes the moment Kennedy reads his landmark opinion:

Kennedy was offering an apology. As he expressed regret for the previous decision that had denied gay men and women the right to make intimate and personal choices, several of the lawyers in the front rows of the courtroom began weeping openly. . . . Kennedy acknowledges that he agonizes over his opinions, but he didn't on that one. The right result was so obvious, he later told Thurgood Marshall's wife, that he wrote the decision over the course of one weekend.[1]

Behind the velvet curtain, Kennedy has been transformed. Like Blackmun in the 70s and 80s and Douglas in the 50s and 60s, Kennedy's story is that of America's gradual understanding and acceptance of gay men and women. These justices not only changed their minds, but changed the course of history in ways that will have deep, lasting consequences for millions. Their personal journeys illuminate the decades-long passage still being taken by societies around the globe to a place where all people, gay and non-gay, are welcomed and embraced.

[1] Jan Crawford Greenburg, *Supreme Conflict: The Inside Story of the Struggle for Control of the United States Supreme Court* (New York: The Penguin Press, 2007), 56-57.

Appendix A contains a detailed outline of each act, including descriptions of central characters, key cases and themes. Appendix B lists confirmed and anticipated on-camera participants.

Structure and Aesthetics

This story demands heavy use of interviews combined with archival materials. The core of the story is told through interviews with many of the individuals who participated directly in the Court's gay rights cases or were close to those who did: former colleagues of Supreme Court justices (including several senior staff who are gay), justices' friends and family members, as well as plaintiffs, defendants and their attorneys. Legal experts, historians, scholars and journalists provide context for understanding the dramatic stories presented in the film and help the audience stay oriented as this decades-long journey unfolds.[2] The substantial use of archival photographs, moving images, documents and sound recordings – much of which has only recently been released to the public – anchors the narrative, bringing the hidden history to life.

The film will combine a traditional, high-production-value approach to on-camera interviews with an expressive and vibrant treatment of still photos, documents, archival moving images and audio recordings. Interview setups will

minimize distractions and rely on conventional framing in order to foreground the speakers, whose stories, memories and commentary are inherently compelling and need no embellishment. Archival materials, on the other hand, will need special treatment in order to be effective. So much of the factual record of this story exists in legal documents, in the handwritten scrawl of justices in private meetings and in scratchy recordings of courtroom arguments. Our challenge is to reveal the most meaningful of these hidden gems in ways that are appropriate for film and truly capture the imaginations of viewers.

The movie will be shot widescreen, in high definition with true cinema lenses, and will have the rich, textured look of film as opposed to the flat, vérité feel more commonly found in video. Aesthetic influences include the classical, chronological storytelling and interview settings of a film such as *Reconstruction: The Second Civil War* (American Experience, 2003); the dramatic and artistic use of archival materials, filmed illustrations and motion graphics in work by Errol Morris, especially *The Fog of War*; and the highly intimate framing sometimes seen in Spike Lee's documentaries (*4 Little Girls*). Documentaries with gay themes are additional important influences: *The Times of Harvey Milk* relies on interviews and archival footage to tell a civil rights story by exploring real human emotion and drama. More recently, *Paragraph 175* illustrates how a film can dynamically and grippingly tackle an issue that is anchored in the law (Germany's anti-gay penal code during the Nazi era).

---

[2] The producers have secured commitments from a wide range of critical contributors, including former Supreme Court staff; senior members of the judiciary; participants and attorneys for major cases; highly regarded analysts and observers such as *The New Yorker's* Jeffrey Toobin and *The New York Times's* Linda Greenhouse; and academics from major law schools and institutes (e.g., Georgetown, U.C. Berkeley).

6

Point of View

It is said that history is written by the victors, but it is equally true that one path to victory is the act of writing our own history. In the case of gay history, we have the added challenge that so much has been hidden. This film will illuminate a history that is largely unknown but of deep significance to LGBT people, our society and our world. Telling the bigger story: America's struggle to find fair treatment for gays in its heart.

For this reason *Eyes on the Prize* stands out as a major influence we hope to emulate. Americans now see the treatment of blacks historically as "just not right," as "inhumane," as "un-American." But this wasn't always our perspective as a society. *Eyes on the Prize* contributed to a broad effort that helped crystallize and ultimately define our understanding of the black civil rights struggle, once and for all removing all doubt about what was perpetrated against blacks, and about the high human cost of prejudice. Works such as *Eyes on the Prize* help to create new norms in our society, which finally comes to see equality as a question of basic fairness, one of our core values as Americans.

The struggle for LGBT equality must be understood in similarly heroic terms. This is not just a fight that belongs to gay men and women. It's a fight that all Americans must embrace as their own,

because ultimately the value we are fighting for is fairness. To this end, the filmmakers have three principles which are guiding development of the project:

John Lawrence and Tyron Garner successfully fight Texas's sodomy law in 2003. As the decision is announced, gay rights advocates weep openly in the courtroom. Justice Antonin Scalia dissents vehemently, declaring the Court has "largely signed on to the so-called homosexual agenda."

(1) By the time viewers finish *Behind the Velvet Curtain*, they will see the treatment of gay men and lesbians, through the experiences of the litigants in the court cases, as fundamentally unfair and unjustifiable. The fight itself will be cast as a question of basic fairness. (You don't have to like someone to be outraged at the sight of their unfair treatment.)

(2) As important, the film will treat the "opponents" of LGBT equality with fairness and compassion. This is not a fight of good versus evil, but one pitting innocence against ignorance. The primary driver of anti-gay efforts, time and again, is revealed to be ignorance. This is as true

for the anti-gay litigants as for the justices who have voted against gay rights. Even if there may be more than ignorance at the heart of some of the deepest animus directed toward gays and lesbians, the vast majority of people who oppose LGBT equality do so out of ignorance and its frequent companion, fear. Simply witness the dramatic discrepancies in attitudes between those who know no gay people versus those who personally know even one openly gay person.

(3) Having framed the conflict as one between innocence and ignorance, what is the dramatic change, the revelation, the revolution the film will present? It is the story of American society going into conflict over homosexuality, becoming aware of the existence of homosexuals, coming to accept their existence, and eventually learning to welcome them as full and equal citizens in our society. It is a story that is reflected within the gay community as gay men and women have come to accept and understand themselves. It is a story seen in microcosm within the Court as an institution. Most importantly, that same story is personified by a handful of justices whose personal journeys lead them to confront their own prejudices and, perhaps to their own surprise, take up the cause of true equality for homosexuals.

Social change happens because people change. The struggle for human rights is, in the end, won by touching hearts and changing minds. *Behind the Velvet Curtain* has the potential to contribute a great deal – not just to the fight for LGBT equality, but for fair and equal treatment for all people.

Audience, Distribution and Digital Media Strategies

The producers have had exploratory discussions with numerous domestic and international distributors and broadcasters who have expressed excitement about the project. We have letters and other explicit indications of interest from senior executives at companies such as Zeitgeist Films, ro*co films, Films Transit, Magnolia Pictures, Channel 4, OutTV (Canada) and others, and we have been encouraged by representatives at Independent Television Service (ITVS) to apply for an R&D grant through their commissioned funding process. An ambitious traditional media distribution plan is complemented by an equally substantial digital media audience engagement strategy.

Behind the Velvet Curtain targets audiences with interests in politics, the law and social justice, as well as people interested in the history of the gay and lesbian movement in the United States. Of clear relevance to gays and lesbians themselves, the film will appeal to mainstream audiences because the stories are first and foremost those of everyday people. The current sociopolitical climate is expanding popular curiosity about both the Supreme Court and the gay experience, but it is the natural drama of the courtroom narrative that will ensure the film reaches even those viewers who might never have considered seeing "a documentary about the Supreme Court" or "a movie about gay rights."

We are focusing on three traditional distribution channels: festival/theatrical release,

Eagle Scout James Dale fights to be reinstated as a scoutmaster after the Boy Scouts of America say they do not allow 'avowed homosexuals as members or leaders.' The Court splits 5-4 against Dale.

television and educational institutions. Gay and lesbian film festivals are an obvious target as are mainstream festivals that include documentaries. Television, however, offers the broadest audience, and the film's high-definition, widescreen format adds to its marketability at a time when the consumer migration to HD is accelerating and providers need quality content in this format. Public broadcasting – via an established series such as P.O.V. – is one potential television distributor and has great reach. Cable channels that program documentaries of this nature include HBO, Showtime, IFC and Sundance as well as more mainstream programmers that are expanding and diversifying their original offerings, such as The History Channel. Niche channels targeting the gay and lesbian market, such as Logo and Here!, also are top distribution candidates.

Educational institutions will fuel the video release of *Behind the Velvet Curtain*, including the more than 200 law schools, nearly 150 university-level American studies and LGBT studies programs and potentially hundreds of high school civics classes. Hundreds of libraries in communities across the country will be able to include in their media catalog one of the only documentaries ever made about the Supreme Court.

Secondary markets for the film include foreign distribution. The heart of *Behind the Velvet Curtain* may be human drama, but the film also offers a glimpse into the inner workings of one of the most important but least understood pillars of American democracy. As gay rights issues come to the fore in countries around the globe, the film's relevance beyond U.S. borders will continue to grow.

Digital Media Strategies

Getting in front of audiences is an important first step, but engaging people is our ultimate objective. To that end, we have budgeted for and are developing an innovative multiplatform package of resources to boost the film's impact across interactive channels — from the web to iPods to cell phones and beyond.

The heart of most compelling stories is character. The people whose journeys are explored in *Behind the Velvet Curtain* are powerful personalities with real-life experiences to rival the best fiction. A major outreach tool for the project will be the creation of brief, character-driven sequences for distribution via the web and other digital platforms. More than simply trailers to promote the film, these digital shorts will offer sketches of the film's most absorbing protagonists — quick profiles to make these people real and build emotional connections with audiences. This experimental approach will maximize the benefits of the web while creating a body of promotional resources that will make the project more appealing to traditional broadcasters.

This project offers tremendous potential for deep, interactive engagement with viewers. Already when we talk about this project we have been struck by how many people feel compelled to share personal stories. For every case that makes it to the Supreme Court, there are hundreds of lower court cases and thousands of everyday occurrences that demonstrate the real-world relevance of the journeys portrayed in *Behind the Velvet Curtain*.

Growth of Overt Homosexuality In City Prompts Wide Concern

PERVERTS CALLED GOVERNMENT PERIL

A 1950 *New York Times* article repeats claims that homosexual 'perverts' have 'infiltrated our Government,' in one of the earliest efforts to tie homosexuality and communism. A page 1 story from 1963 frets about 'overt homosexuality.'

10

We envision not only a set of online resources, but a space where people can offer experiences, discuss feelings and become part of a larger societal dialog.

Furthermore, the collected electronic resources will give viewers, teachers and students access to a wide range of artifacts and analysis too lengthy and elaborate to include in the film. The artifacts promise an opportunity to "discover history" directly, unfiltered by others (including the filmmakers). These objects include original legal documents from the court cases, recordings of oral arguments at the Supreme Court, copies of justices' notes, photographs related to the cases, and oral histories and interviews with the men and women who bravely stood up for their rights before the highest court in the land. While a majority of these items are in the public domain, they are not today easily accessible. By gathering these resources and making them available to virtually anyone, we will certainly contribute to independent study, exploration and discovery.

Archival resources are supplemented by interviews with attorneys, clerks, historians and analysts – fuller versions of the interviews presented in the film. *Behind the Velvet Curtain* especially lends itself to this type of comprehensive informational supplement because of its sweeping timeframe and the civic nature of its topic. The film and its web- and DVD-based collection will serve as an incredible real-world lesson on the inner workings of the Supreme Court.

One of the most exciting ideas we are exploring is a potential partnership with the UCLA Williams Institute on sexual orientation and the law, which would repurpose the film and its archival materials for use in Continuing Legal Education for active attorneys, prosecutors and public defenders, and members of the judiciary. This is a way to reach people in positions of influence – people who, like the justices portrayed in the film, are being called to examine and challenge their own prejudices.

We believe there are many other innovative ways to market the film and engage audiences, and we are committed to building those strategies concurrent with production.

'As long as they don't want to flaunt their homosexuality, they have equal rights the same as anyone else,' argues pop singer and orange juice spokesperson Anita Bryant, leading a nationwide campaign to ban gay teachers from the classroom.

11

Budget and Fundraising Plan

Behind the Velvet Curtain is an ambitious project, sweeping in scope and complex in execution. To realize the project's full potential as the definitive document of a generations-long legal struggle for gay rights, a major investment is required. We believe the funding outlook is bright for this timely and important project.

The project will necessitate extensive research followed by travel to interview dozens of litigants, attorneys, clerks, judges, historians and analysts. A high shooting ratio is essential for a story that spans six decades and has such a large "cast." (Select footage not used in the final cut will constitute much of the digital media resources accompanying the film.) Additionally, heavy use of archival documents, images and recordings is projected to require a significant front-end investment for research, plus post-production expense for clearance. The high-definition format also adds some cost, although the producers believe this will be more than offset by the project's enhanced marketability.

Recognizing the risks inherent with any film project, and with documentaries in particular, the production team is deferring a majority of their compensation in order to reduce cash required to complete the project. The attached expense budget (Appendix C) details the full-cost for each line item, as well as expected in-kind support and deferrals. A standard contingency of ten percent has been added.

Taking into account deferrals, the project will require approximately $1 million for production plus another $250,000

for digital media strategies and outreach, to be raised from the following sources:

Individual supporters		
	Direct marketing	$35,000
	Events (8)	$100,000
	Major donors ($1,000+)	$150,000
		$285,000
Corporations (including in-kind)		$50,000
Other in-kind support		$15,000
Foundation grants		
	Film/arts funders	$400,000
	LGBT funders	$120,000
	Other (law, social justice, etc.)	$120,000
		$640,000
Distributors/Broadcasters		$250,000
TOTAL		**$1,250,000**

Producer Robert Martin has worked for more than a decade as a marketing and management consultant to nonprofit or-

142

ganizations and foundations, including some of the country's largest funders. This experience has informed the development of a comprehensive fundraising plan, relying on tried-and-true strategies and the standard 80/20 pyramid approach to raising money (20 percent of the film's funders will account for 80 percent of the money raised).

Several factors contribute to this film's marketability. The Supreme Court is an institution in flux, with a precarious balance almost certain to shift as a result of the 2008 Presidential election. This creates an urgency that can be leveraged in fundraising. Since the 2000 national election and the war in Iraq, the U.S. has witnessed a groundswell of political activism as well as a shift in the way media are being used to influence discourse. *Fahrenheit 9/11, Outfoxed, An Inconvenient Truth, No End in Sight* and other documentaries are demonstrating to savvy donors that independent media can bring information and insights directly to the people.

The film also has several natural constituencies with the means to generate significant funds, including the LGBT

community, and lesbian and gay lawyers in particular. Legal defense and advocacy groups such as Lambda Legal and the National Center for Lesbian Rights rank among the most prominent and well-funded LGBT organizations – an indicator of this community's recognition that the courts are a vital front in the push for equality. Civil and human rights proponents will grasp the movie's importance and will direct their support to help fulfill its potential.

Behind the Velvet Curtain has been in development for more than two years. To date, the producers have raised more than $40,000 from individual donors and another $15,000 in grants from the California Council for the Humanities and the Lucius and Eva Eastman Fund. Although a few key interviews have been shot, full-scale production on the film will require $400,000. The producers plan to begin production in 2009. Principal photography will take six months and post-production eight months, with the ultimate timeframe dependent on funding.

14

The Filmmakers

Behind the Velvet Curtain is conceived, produced and directed by Jonathan Joiner and Robert H. Martin, who bring a valuable combination of filmmaking, legal, fundraising and project management expertise to the project. Together with co-producer Beth Pielert (assistant director for *The Corporation* and producer/director of *Out of the Poison Tree*) they lead a number of experienced filmmakers who are helping to develop the film. Additionally, the producers have formal working relationships with several American history, cultural studies and legal scholars who are supporting content development.

Jonathan Joiner (Producer/Director) is a filmmaker and attorney with a longstanding interest in LGBT rights. Born and raised in Florence, Alabama, he has a commitment to social justice that is informed not just by his experience as a gay man, but through direct exposure to the legacy of segregation in the American South. Jonathan moved to California in the early 90s and has spent the last 16 years in San Francisco. He was deputy director of the H.I.V./AIDS Reentry and Empowerment Project at New College of California, where he earned his J.D. A personal passion for film and film history has driven Jonathan's interest in copyright and intellectual property law, including the theory and application of fair use doctrine in documentary filmmaking. A former student of the Bay Area Video Coalition's video production program, he is a skilled still photographer whose practical experience with lighting, composition and color informs his filmmaking. *Behind the Velvet Curtain* is Jonathan's first film.

Robert Martin (Producer/Director) is a San Francisco-based writer and filmmaker with a passion for politics and longstanding dedication to community improvement. He has worked more than a decade as a communications and strategy consultant in both nonprofit and private sector environments. Since 2001 Robert has been a consultant to Q Media Partners, a Bay Area television production company dedicated to developing "intelligent and entertaining" programming for national distribution. (The company has had first-look deals at HBO and Touchstone, and projects in development at ABC and United Artists.) Exposed to filmmaking through his dad's Super 8 home movies, Robert produced his first film in high school: a documentary exposé triggered by the drug-related arrests of 18 students by an undercover police officer who had posed as an enrolled student. Robert is a Phi Beta Kappa graduate of Reed College, and has completed video production coursework at Portland's Northwest Film Center and the Bay Area Video Coalition.

Beth (Basa) Pielert (Co-Producer) is a director, cinematographer and editor specializing in social justice documentary film. Beth was assistant director and primary camera operator for *The Corporation* miniseries, which garnered dozens of awards including the 2004 Sundance Audience Award. Beth helped shoot *Girls Rock!*, now in theaters, and she co-edited the PBS series *Building Green*. Her first film as director, *Kiss My Cleats*, is a documentary about the 1998 Gay Games. It toured dozens of festivals and is used to teach tolerance in high schools throughout the U.S. In 2007 she completed her feature *Out of the Poison Tree*, an exploration of personal justice and reconciliation for survivors of the Cambodian genocide. The film was licensed by the Center for Asian American Media, aired on PBS and released on Netflix in 2008. Beth's film company is Good Film Works, where in addition to documentary film production she directs/shoots and edits high-definition films for Apple.

Marta Wohl (Editor) is a San Francisco–based editor, producer and story consultant. She has over 20 years experience editing for broadcast, corporate and independent media. She specializes in editing thought-provoking, social-issue documentaries. The films she has edited have won numerous awards, appeared nationally on PBS, and have screened at festivals worldwide. Recently Marta worked for four years in the documentary unit at LucasFilm, editing 25 of the 94 companion documentaries for *The Adventures of Young Indiana Jones* series. The 22-DVD set was released by LucasFilm and Paramount Pictures in 2008. Marta is passionate about telling powerful stories through great editing, and has

strong collaborative skills. She has produced, written and edited her own documentaries. As an Avid Certified Instructor from 1994 to 2003, she taught hundreds of editors basic to advanced editing techniques. Her five-year stint as staff editor in a high-end post-production facility helps her bring a high degree of technical knowledge to any project.

Sinisa Kukic (Cinematographer) is a film and video photographer with a diverse background in documentary, narrative and experimental projects. A graduate of Southern Illinois University with a B.A. in cinema and photography, he has an M.F.A. from San Francisco State University. His film *Breathe* (2003) aired on Fox Television and his undergraduate thesis, *Conduit Of Displacement* (2004), won the Loren D. Cocking Animation Award. *Pump* (2006), his most recent film, explores the hybridization of the bicycle and the cyclist and has screened at over a dozen international film festivals and on PBS. His preoccupation with the particulars of camera carriage and movement is rooted in his involvement in the local biking community and his work as a racecar mechanic. Born in the former Yugoslavia, Kukic and his family moved to Chicago when he was eleven. He currently resides in Los Angeles, where he is editing *Imaginary Lines*, a documentary about migrant border crossings in Arizona.

Mark Page (Script Consultant) has worked since 1985 as a producer, writer, co-producer, associate producer and researcher on over forty documentary projects for PBS, Fox Television, Turner Broadcasting and JAK Films/LucasFilm Ltd/Paramount Pictures. Mark was associate producer of

16

the Academy Award-nominated *Super Chief: The Life and Legacy of Earl Warren*, a 90-minute PBS biography of the late chief justice that earned him a national Emmy Award nomination for Outstanding Achievement in Research. Mark has 18 titles as a producer and writer for LucasFilm and has contributed to dozens of projects for PBS, including *Stopwatch*, a biography of pioneering efficiency expert Frederick Winslow Taylor; *Naked To The Bone*, a history of medical imaging; *What About God?*, a look at America's ongoing struggles over evolution and creationism that was the final episode in the WGBH-TV series *Evolution*; and *The Next Big Thing*, a special looking at the history of technology to seek insights into its future.

17

Appendix A: The Story

The project has natural divisions into three parts, each of which corresponds to a discrete period of American social and political history, gay rights history and Court history. Each discrete act links with the other two to form a single, comprehensive chronicle of the gay rights fight at the high court.

Act I: "1953 – 1969: Faggots Stay Out"

Act I is about the emergence of a visible homosexual minority and society's attempts to keep that minority silent.

In the wake of World War II, the U.S. assumes a central place on the world stage as a superpower whose moral authority is based largely on our advocacy of human rights, while an increasingly fragmented and divided society challenges our own commitment to these principles. By the time the Supreme Court ends school segregation, in 1954, it has come to be seen as the ultimate defender of human rights and a refuge for those whom the majority would otherwise oppress. This is the context in which society and the high court first come face to face with "the homosexual problem."

Our story begins in the 1950s and 60s, when the nation is confronted by the existence of a homosexual population which is beginning to find its voice – a voice so threatening, it must be silenced. Under J. Edgar Hoover's watchful eye, the F.B.I. and

Homosexual activists picket the White House in 1965, protesting government witch hunts to root out homosexuals. They include Frank Kameny (center-left, in gray suit), who was the first homosexual to petition the Supreme Court in an effort to save his job.

the United States Post Office mobilize to shut down the first national gay magazine, deeming the mere discussion of homosexuality obscene. Vice units at police departments around the country begin identifying "sex deviates" and feeding their names to the F.B.I. and I.N.S., who in turn use this information to have homosexuals fired or deported. By the 60s, law enforcement is using hidden cameras, undercover agents and outright brutality to root out and eradicate "perverts."

The Supreme Court, like society at large, struggles to figure out what to make of homosexuals and homosexuality. Under chief justice Earl Warren, this Court advances protections for racial minorities but is baffled by the new problems posed by homosexuals. Court documents, notes taken by justices during private conferences and discussions recounted by clerks and family members reveal awkward attempts to come to grips with homosexuality. Is homosexuality a disease? A contagion that can be spread? A moral weakness? A criminal behavior? These questions are at the core of the cases the Court is asked to resolve: Should homosexuals be allowed to have their own magazine? Can the government fire someone for "immorality?" Should homosexual immigrants be denied citizenship and deported? Are homosexuals so degenerate, so dangerous as to justify brutal police tactics to drive them out of communities?

One justice emerges as a central player in Act I. William Douglas is a maverick – a Pacific Northwesterner with a cowboy's live-and-let-live approach to life. Nicknamed Wild Bill both for his judicial tactics and his pioneer spirit, he retreats each summer to his ranch in Washington State, where he builds a decades-long friendship with his neighbors, a lesbian couple. It is Douglas who emerges as the Supreme Court's first defender of homosexuals. In 1967, when the Court permits the I.N.S. to deport homosexuals as persons "afflicted with psychopathic personality," Douglas writes out a passionate dissent in his own hand. Yet even among allies, the "enlightened" view stings: homosexuals deserve our pity, not our condemnation.

By the late 60s, over Douglas's objections, the Court has endorsed society's efforts to silence homosexuals, labeling them psychopaths, moral degenerates and outlaws. Ohio men convicted of sodomy – the lucky ones sentenced to 20-year prison terms, others facing lifetime confinement in state mental institutions – get no hearing at the high court; Douglas is the lone vote to take the case. The Court ignores the plight of men and women beaten by Los Angeles police outside two gay bars on New Year's Eve 1966 – one man clubbed so badly he loses his spleen; again, Douglas alone

wishes to intervene. The Court's indifference is clear. For homosexuals, there is no refuge offered here.

Act II: "1969 – 1986: Flaunting It"

In Act II the closet doors are kicked down. No longer on the defensive, gays push for basic freedoms. A society – and a Court – that spent decades trying to silence the homosexual voice and smother the nascent homosexual movement is now faced with activists demanding equality.

As Act II begins, the Supreme Court, the country and the gay community are all experiencing major change. Although gays have learned firsthand that the Court will turn a blind eye to injustices perpetrated against them, the popular impression is of a liberal, activist Court. Chief Justice Earl Warren's retirement begins two years of political maneuvering to control the next Court, and Nixon's promise to move the Court to the right becomes a cornerstone of his Presidential campaign. Liberal Justice Abe Fortas is forced out by scandal, and William Douglas narrowly escapes an impeachment attempt by Congressional Republicans. Nixon appointees Warren Burger and Harry Blackmun are confirmed with the expectation they will take the Court in a conservative, law-and-order direction.

The turmoil on the Court during late 60s and early 70s parallels that of American society. Gays are part of this change. After 1966's bloody New Year's Eve bar raid in Los Angeles, homosexuals led peaceful public protests. Two and a half

20

The Court's newest justice, Nixon appointee Harry Blackmun, arrives unlikely to sympathize with gay causes. In his first Supreme Court gay rights case, Blackmun views the plaintiff's openness about his homosexuality as a reason to vote against him. The man, who loses his job after his employer learns he applied for a marriage license with his male partner, must be a troublemaker. Why else would he be public about being gay? Why else would he attempt to marry another man? Blackmun's private notes reveal concern not for the man who was fired, but for the employer who wants no association with a gay person. In another case, Blackmun joins future Chief Justice William Rehnquist, arguing that universities should be allowed to ban gay student groups for the same reasons they would quarantine measles-sufferers: to prevent the spread of contagion.

Meanwhile, a stronger gay movement coalesces and for the first time develops a legal strategy for promoting gay rights. Activists look at the cases they've lost and realize that the underlying issue – the trump card for the anti-gay litigants – has been the argument that homosexuals are appropriately singled out for discrimination because they are criminals. It's OK to deny a job or citizenship to someone who espouses crime. It's OK to refuse recognition of student groups that promote crime, and to keep criminals out of our classrooms, away from our children. It's OK to deny custody to parents who commit crimes. Gay legal activists realize they are always going to be on the losing side unless they can gut the laws that define homosexuals as criminals. They begin looking for a case to challenge those laws.

years later, when police raid the Stonewall Inn bar in New York, gays fight back forcefully and riot for several nights. The message is clear: Gays are no longer going to take abuse quietly. In growing numbers, gays are coming out and standing up for their rights.

Suddenly, Americans discover they have gay coworkers and neighbors, that there are gay students and teachers, gay churchgoers and political activists. The growing presence of openly gay men and women leads to conflict. We see employers firing people for being openly gay. Newspapers refuse to run ads for gay discussion groups, and universities deny recognition to gay student groups. A highly visible, nationwide campaign to root out gay school teachers is spearheaded by Christian pop singer Anita Bryant. These confrontations inevitably end up at the Court.

Still other, more basic survival issues are being faced by gay men and women. An American and his Australian lover, whose church marriage goes unrecognized by the I.N.S., desperately seek a way to prevent the Australian's imminent deportation. "You have failed to establish that a bona fide marital relationship can exist between two faggots," writes an I.N.S. official. Across the country another long-term couple is torn apart by tragedy: After her partner is struck by a drunk driver and left severely incapacitated, a woman spends eight years fighting for the right to see and care for her lover, against the wishes of family members who do not recognize their relationship. These cases, too, find their way to the high court.

Inside the Court there are radically different approaches to gay cases in the chambers of different justices – and growing conflict within the Court. Throughout the '70s and early 80s, battle lines have been drawn and a complex game of chess has begun behind the velvet curtain. Every petition and appeal to the Court relating to sodomy sets in motion maneuvering by justices and their clerks to manipulate the outcomes – and in most instances the Court simply refuses to hear those cases. "I'm not sure the world is ready for this one," a clerk notes about an early '70s petition in a case where a man has been sentenced to 20 years in prison for consensual sodomy. A decade later another case prompts a more ominous response in a private note: "Taking this case could be a disaster... the heat of the Moral Majority would fall upon the Court... let the matter die." Caught between liberal and conservative blocs are justices such as Lewis Powell, whose papers reveal hand-wringing and discomfort over any issue relating to sex and sexuality, and Blackmun, whose personal belief that homosexuality is immoral has begun to clash with the principles of personal freedom he has articulated in defend abortion rights.

Then *Bowers v. Hardwick* arrives. A Georgia man is fighting his arrest, in his own bedroom, for oral sex. The justices agonize over whether or not to accept the case, and during a one-week period three of them switch their votes on whether to hear it – one justice flip-flopping twice. Liberal William Brennan initially votes to take the case, but Blackmun urges him privately to reverse his position, fearing that a conservative win on sodomy would undermine fundamental aspects of Blackmun's *Roe v. Wade* abortion decision. Brennan

quickly switches his vote to refuse the case, but Chief Justice Burger suddenly reverses his own original position – he has been doing his own math and has realized *Hardwick* offers a very real chance of a milestone conservative victory.

Two days after the case is argued, the justices assemble for their private conference, where even reliably liberal votes are on the line. "I have a bias," admits John Paul Stevens, "but we have to live with this." Lewis Powell surprises his colleagues and votes to overturn Georgia's sodomy law, arguing it unfairly punishes homosexuals for behavior they cannot control. But one day later the Chief Justice hand-delivers an extraordinary private letter to Powell, pressing him to change his vote. The head of the nation's highest court writes: "Are those with an 'orientation' towards rape to be let off merely because they allege that the act of rape is 'irresistible' to them? Are we to excuse every 'Jack the Ripper?'" Days later Powell sends a memo to his colleagues announcing he has switched his position. Gay rights groups don't yet know it, but they've just lost the most important Supreme Court case in gay rights history.

Willfully ignoring the fact that Georgia's sodomy law applies equally to heterosexuals and homosexuals, the Court's opinion singles out gays, saying there is "no fundamental right to engage in homosexual sodomy" and citing "millennia of moral teaching ... firmly rooted in Judeo-Christian moral and ethical standards." Harry Blackmun – the man who 15 years earlier viewed being openly gay as justification for losing one's job – pens a passionate dissent and reads it from the bench to underscore the case's importance. Black-

22

mun's transformation is remarkable: he is now the Court's most ardent champion of gay rights. *Hardwick*, he says, is about "the right most valued by civilized men,' namely, 'the right to be let alone."

The next morning every major paper carries the news across the top of its front page. Gay rights groups are faced with a devastating loss. Not only have sodomy laws not been gutted, they have been reinforced. Four years later Justice Powell says publicly that he "probably made a mistake." But there are no do-overs at the Supreme Court. The tribunal has ruled: there are no gay rights in the Constitution.

Act III: "1986 – 2008: A Place At The Table"

In Act III, efforts to exclude homosexuals from American society are stepped up. The country, forced to acknowledge the existence of homosexuals, is saying, "We don't have to accept you as equals." But the tide turns. Anti-gay forces overreach, and the Court begins to discern the animus fueling their attacks. The Court admits its mistake in Hardwick and reverses itself, beginning its slow turn toward full equality for gay Americans.

Act III begins with the Reagan Revolution in full swing. AIDS is crippling the gay community, and the outlook is bleak. Gays have suffered their biggest legal defeat. The movement's activists and legal strategists are in disarray. The *Hardwick* loss virtually ensures homosexuality will remain criminalized for at least another generation. The Court has sent a clear message – to the gay community and to its

opponents – that it is willing to accept second-class treatment for homosexuals.

Anti-gay forces mobilize to capitalize on their win in *Hardwick*. Efforts are increased to block gays from living as integrated members of American society: St. Patrick's Day parade organizers refuse to march with Irish homosexuals. Boy Scout troupes purge known gay people from their ranks. The U.S. Olympic Committee blocks homosexuals from staging the "Gay Olympics." Over the course of just a few years these three highly public cases come to the Court. The country is struggling to come to terms with the presence of gay people – and the country is saying, "there's no place for you at our table." The gay community loses every one of these cases.

Meanwhile, the Court turns further right. Chief Justice Burger retires, giving Reagan the opportunity to elevate William Rehnquist to head the Court and appoint Antonin Scalia to the vacancy. Lewis Powell, the deciding vote in *Hardwick*, continues as the swing vote that never seems to swing in favor of homosexuals. One year after *Hardwick* and one day after his majority opinion denying gays the right to use the word "Olympics," Powell announces his departure from the Court and sets in motion one of the most famous series of confirmation battles in history. Reagan's nomination of arch-conservative Robert Bork ultimately is defeated in the Senate by eight votes, and his next pick, Douglas Ginsburg, withdraws in controversy over marijuana use. Reagan makes his third choice: Anthony Kennedy.

Who is Anthony Kennedy? Gay rights groups fear the worst after discovering that this former Boy Scout and Catholic altar boy has a solidly anti-gay record as a lower-court judge. Kennedy has upheld military policies banning gays, ruled that employers were justified in firing workers who "flaunt" homosexuality, and even upheld statutes punishing homosexual rape more harshly than heterosexual rape. Despite concerns voiced by liberal groups, Kennedy is confirmed unanimously.

Over the next three years the Court's most outspoken liberals, William Brennan and Thurgood Marshall, succumb to illness and retire. Bush's replacements leave the nine-member Court with exactly one justice appointed by a Democrat: Byron White, author of the *Hardwick* gay rights defeat. Emboldened, gay rights opponents push for increasingly restrictive policies meant to circumscribe protections for gays. In 1992 Colorado passes Amendment 2, a law of unprecedented scope which would have blocked any and all claims of unfair treatment on the basis of sexual orientation. At once vague and sweeping, the law has one clear purpose: to put the state on record that it will stand by and permit discrimination against homosexuals.

After Colorado's high court blocks enforcement of the law and anti-gay forces appeal, the U.S. Supreme Court steps in and signals its intention to issue its own, controlling ruling. The possibility that Amendment 2 could be upheld is nothing short of terrifying to gay legal advocates, who understand its potential to leave gay men and lesbians truly powerless to fight discrimination through the courts. A loss in this case would, once and for all, mean that the gay rights legal fight had been lost.

In the courtroom on the morning of oral arguments, anxious observers sit up when less than a minute into the presentation Anthony Kennedy interrupts the lawyer who is arguing in favor of Amendment 2. The Reagan appointee with the anti-gay voting record states, "I've never seen a case like this." "That was the moment in the case," remembers one of O'Connor's clerks who was in the audience. It is as if gay rights opponents have overreached so egregiously that Kennedy is forced to recognize their motivation for what it is: pure animus. In the end, it is Kennedy who writes for a six-vote majority: "Amendment 2 classifies homosexuals not to further a proper legislative end but to make them unequal to everyone else. This Colorado cannot do. A State cannot so deem a class of persons a stranger to its laws."

A major bullet has been dodged. But the Amendment 2 win does not resolve most of the gay rights issues – it simply preserves the right to ask the courts for help. Although the Court appears to have drawn a line, a lot of anti-gay discrimination remains permissible. In Pennsylvania a man is not only fired for being gay but ordered to pay more than $100,000 in damages for breaching his employment contract, which had listed homosexuality as grounds for dismissal. In Georgia an employer fires a woman and justifies it not because she is a lesbian, but because her marriage to another woman in a private religious ceremony would negatively impact "public perception." Both cases are turned away, illus-

24

152

trating the Court's ongoing reluctance to take on gay rights cases.

Yet in 2003 Kennedy once again surprises observers by spearheading the Court's extraordinary decision to review and reverse the *Hardwick* ruling, in what becomes the gay community's biggest legal win: *Lawrence v. Texas*. The 2003 ruling repeals all sodomy laws, homosexual and heterosexual, and has implications for everything from same-sex marriage to the future of "don't ask, don't tell." Journalist Jan Crawford Greenburg describes the moment when Kennedy reads his landmark opinion:

Kennedy was offering an apology. As he expressed regret for the previous decision that had denied gay men and women the right to make intimate and personal choices, several of the lawyers in the front rows of the courtroom began weeping openly. . . . Kennedy acknowledges that he

agonizes over his opinions, but he didn't on that one. The right result was so obvious, he later told Thurgood Marshall's wife, that he wrote the decision over the course of one weekend.

Anthony Kennedy had come to the Court with a record suggesting he was at best ambivalent about gay rights. Behind the velvet curtain, however, he was transformed. Kennedy, like Blackmun in the 70s and 80s and William Douglas in the 50s and 60s, had become an unlikely hero in the story of America's gradual acceptance of gay men and women. These justices not only changed their minds, but changed the course of history in ways that will have deep, lasting consequences for millions of Americans. The personal journeys of these justices, in the end, illuminate the decades-long passage still being taken by American society to a place where all people, gay and non-gay, are welcomed and embraced.

25

Appendix B: Interview Subjects

The producers anticipate including segments from interviews with approximately 40 subjects. Of those, three or four are likely to be big-picture commentators, able to guide the viewer through the decades-long story. Additionally, each act will feature roughly 12 to 15 subjects whose expertise or experiences are relevant to the specific time period in question: former clerks and Court employees who served during particular terms, family members and colleagues of justices, attorneys who litigated before the Court, historians and legal analysts, and, of course, wherever possible, the gay men and lesbians whose lives were so deeply affected by Court decisions.

The producers have made contact with and secured preliminary commitments from a number of potential interview subjects, including former Supreme Court clerks who worked during terms where gay rights cases came before the Court. Several of the clerks who have agreed to cooperate are in fact people who drafted landmark high court opinions and dissents for their bosses on landmark gay rights issues.

One of our most ambitious hopes is to interview a living justice, either retired or sitting: Sandra Day O'Connor and Anthony Kennedy top the list. Although the project certainly does not depend on access to the justices, the possibility of hearing directly from the ultimate insiders is tantalizing, and we are consulting with former *New York Times* reporter Linda Greenhouse to develop a strategy for securing an interview with a justice. There is little precedent for justices – especially those who are active on the bench – to grant interviews for a project such as *Behind the Velvet Curtain*. Under Chief Justice John Roberts, however, the justices have been giving much greater access to the media than during

the Rehnquist years. In the last year, in addition to frequent appearances on C-SPAN, justices have granted interviews for a documentary series produced for PBS, a documentary feature film aired on HBO, and even a Sunday morning newsmaker program on Fox News.

Because the project will rely so heavily on interviews, it matters a great deal not just what is said but how those ideas are communicated. The selection of subjects is most appropriately viewed as casting, and a significant part of pre-production will be devoted to advance interviews and screen tests.

The categories from which we will draw interview subjects, with selected examples of people whose participation we have solicited or will be soliciting, include:

Litigants and Attorneys from Both Sides of Key Cases: We have identified more than two dozen living litigants and attorneys, from the very first gay rights Supreme Court case

Historians and Other Academics: David A. J. Richards (*The Case for Gay Rights*); John D'Emilio (*Sexual Politics, Sexual Communities*); Ronald Bayer (*Homosexuality and American Psychiatry*); Kenji Yoshino (*Covering The Hidden Assault on Our Civil Rights*).

Other Public Personalities: Anti-gay campaigner Anita Bryant; Congressional Representative Barney Frank.

Former Clerks, Court Employees and Justices' Family Members: Philip Heymann (clerk for John Marshall Harlan II, now at Harvard Law School); Cathy Douglas Stone (widow of William Douglas); Rory Little (clerk for William Brennan); Wanda Martinson (Harry Blackmun's secretary); Harold Koh (Blackmun clerk and dean of Yale Law School); Cabell Chinnis (Lewis Powell's gay clerk during *Hardwick*); Pam Karlan (Blackmun's clerk for *Hardwick*, now at Stanford Law School); David Sklansky (former Blackmun clerk, now professor at U.C. Berkeley School of Law); Bill Hohengarten (former clerk for David Souter and attorney on *Lawrence*).

in the 1950s through those of recent years. A number of critical participants are in their 80s; we have a narrowing window of opportunity to capture their eyewitness accounts of gay history-in-the-making.

Journalists and Court Observers: Author Lisa keen (*Strangers to the Law*); *New York Times* reporter Linda Greenhouse (*Becoming Justice Blackmun*); ABC News correspondent Jan Crawford Greenburg (*Supreme Conflict*); NPR correspondent Nina Totenberg; Bob Woodward (*The Brethren*), Edward Lazarus (*Closed Chambers*); *New Yorker* writer Jeffrey Toobin (*The Nine Inside the Secret World of the Supreme Court*).

Biographers: Bruce Allen Murphy (*Wild Bill: The Legend and Life of William O. Douglas*); John Jeffries (*Justice Lewis F. Powell: A Biography*); Joan Biskupic (*Sandra Day O'Connor: How the First Woman on the Supreme Court Became its Most Influential Justice*), Dennis Hutchinson (*The Man Who Once Was Whizzer White: A Portrait of Justice Byron R. White*).

Gay Rights Advocates and Strategists: Kate Kendall (National Center for Lesbian Rights); Evan Wolfson (Freedom to Marry, Lambda Legal Defense & Education Fund); Laurence Tribe (Harvard Law School).

28

Appendix C: Project Advisors

The producers have formal working relationships with several American history, cultural studies and legal scholars and are working informally with many others. These experts have agreed to review and contribute to development of a detailed treatment and script for the project, as well as assist in developing guides for interviewing participants in the cases. They also will support analysis of the interview findings and interpretation of additional field and archival research. Additionally, several experienced filmmakers are advising the project. A partial listing of advisors follows.

Peter Calabrese
Chief Executive Officer, Q Media Partners

Jon W. Davidson, Esq.
Legal Director, Lambda Legal

Chai R. Feldblum, J.D.
Director, Federal Legislation Clinic; Professor of Law
Georgetown University

Nan Hunter, J.D.
Legal Scholarship Director
The Williams Institute, UCLA School of Law

Kate Kendell, Esq.
Executive Director, National Center for Lesbian Rights

Craig Loftin, Ph.D.
Lecturer, Department of American Studies
California State University, Fullerton

Thom Lynch
Consultant and Former Executive Director,
San Francisco LGBT Community Center

Martin Meeker, Ph.D.
Academic Specialist, University of California, Berkeley

Mark Page
Filmmaker – *Super Chief The Life and Legacy of Earl Warren* (Associate Producer); *What About God?*, WGBH (Writer)

David A. Sklansky, J.D.
Professor of Law; Faculty Co-Chair,
Berkeley Center for Criminal Justice
University of California, Berkeley, School of Law

Sharon Wood
Filmmaker – *Paragraph 175* (Writer); *The Celluloid Closet* (Story)

Appendix D: Comprehensive Budget

Summary

CATEGORY/ LINE ITEM	Pre-Production	Production	Post-Production	PRODUCTION TOTAL	Distribution	GRAND TOTAL
1.00 PERSONNEL						
Sub-Total	180,000	238,000	339,400	757,400	196,880	954,280
In-Kind	1,000	-	-	1,000	58,500	59,500
Deferred	137,700	79,250	101,500	318,450	-	318,450
Cash Needed	41,300	158,750	237,900	437,950	138,380	576,330
2.00 EQUIPMENT RENTAL						
Sub-Total	725	113,350	10,000	124,075	1,500	125,575
In-Kind	725	-	-	725	-	725
Deferred	-	-	-	-	-	-
Cash Needed	-	113,350	10,000	123,350	1,500	124,850
3.00 TRAVEL						
Sub-Total	25,700	115,530	-	141,230	11,500	152,730
In-Kind	5,000	6,760	-	11,760	1,000	12,760
Deferred	-	-	-	-	-	-
Cash Needed	20,700	108,770	-	129,470	10,500	139,970
4.00 MATERIALS & SERVICES						
Sub-Total	8,400	22,500	139,400	170,300	26,400	196,700
In-Kind	-	-	-	-	-	-
Deferred	-	-	-	-	-	-
Cash Needed	8,400	22,500	139,400	170,300	26,400	196,700
5.00 ADMINISTRATIVE						
Sub-Total	14,060	8,780	6,780	29,620	12,800	42,420
In-Kind	-	-	-	-	-	-
Deferred	10,560	2,840	-	13,200	-	13,200
Cash Needed	3,500	6,140	6,780	16,420	12,800	29,220
6.00 INSURANCE						
Sub-Total	-	20,000	7,500	27,500	-	27,500
In-Kind	-	-	-	-	-	-
Deferred	-	-	-	-	-	-
Cash Needed	-	20,000	7,500	27,500	-	27,500

CATEGORY / LINE ITEM	Pre-Production	Production	Post-Production	PRODUCTION TOTAL	Distribution	GRAND TOTAL
SUB-TOTAL						
Sub-Total	**228,885**	**518,160**	**503,080**	**1,250,125**	**249,080**	**1,499,205**
In-Kind	6,725	6,760	-	13,485	59,500	72,985
Deferred	148,260	81,890	101,500	331,650	-	331,650
Cash Needed	73,900	429,510	401,580	904,990	189,580	1,094,570
CONTINGENCY (10%)	7,390	42,951	40,158	90,499	18,958	109,457
TOTAL CASH NEEDED	81,290	472,461	441,738	$ 995,489	208,538	$1,204,027

Pre-Production
TIMEFRAME: 12 months

CATEGORY/LINE ITEM	Amount	Units	Rate	Sub-Total	In-Kind	Deferred	Cash Needed
1.00 PERSONNEL							
1.10 Producer/director (Joiner)	12	months	5,000	60,000	-	60,000	-
1.11 Producer/director (Martin)	12	months	5,000	60,000	-	60,000	-
1.12 Co-producer/line producer	24	days	400	9,600	-	4,800	4,800
1.13 Executive producer(s)	1	allow	10,000	10,000	-	5,000	5,000
1.14 Writer(s)	2	weeks	2,500	5,000	-	2,500	2,500
1.30 Production mgr	6	weeks	1,800	10,800	-	5,400	5,400
1.31 Office assistant/intern	120	hours	15	1,800	-	-	1,800
1.50 Graduate researcher	40	days	250	10,000	-	-	10,000
1.51 Research intern	60	days	75	4,500	-	-	4,500
1.52 Archival researcher	8	days	350	2,800	-	-	2,800
1.90 Consultants	40	hours	75	3,000	1,000	-	2,000
1.91 Scholar stipends	1	allow	2,500	2,500	-	-	2,500
Total Personnel				180,000	1,000	137,700	41,300
2.00 EQUIPMENT RENTAL							
2.40 Digital still camera	1	camera	225	225	225		
2.41 Document/image scanner	1	scanner	500	500	500		
Total Equipment				725	725		
3.00 TRAVEL							
3.10 Airfare	20	RT tickets	500	10,000	1,500	-	8,500
3.20 Per diem	60	person-days	45	2,700	-	-	2,700
3.30 Accommodation	30	nights	300	9,000	3,000	-	6,000
3.40 Ground transport	20	trips	200	4,000	500	-	3,500
Total Travel				25,700	5,000		20,700
4.00 MATERIALS & SERVICES							
4.50 Fiscal sponsorship	1	allow	4,900	4,900	-	-	4,900
4.60 Accounting	1	allow	1,000	1,000	-	-	1,000
4.70 Legal	1	allow	500	500	-	-	500
4.80 Promotion	1	allow	2,000	2,000	-	-	2,000
Total Materials & Services				8,400			8,400

	CATEGORY/LINE ITEM	Amount	Units	Rate	Sub-Total	In-Kind	Deferred	Cash Needed
5.00	**ADMINISTRATIVE**							
5.10	Office rental [incl. computers]	12	months	800	9,600	-	9,600	-
5.20	Internet/telecom	12	months	80	960	-	960	-
5.30	Photocopying/printing	1	allow	2,000	2,000	-	-	2,000
5.40	Postage/shipping	1	allow	1,000	1,000	-	-	1,000
5.50	Misc office expenses	1	allow	500	500	-	-	500
	Total Administrative				14,060	-	10,560	3,500
	PRE-PRODUCTION SUB-TOTAL				*228,885*	*6,725*	*148,260*	*73,900*
	CONTINGENCY [estimated @ 10% of cash costs]							*7,390*
	TOTAL PRE-PRODUCTION						$	**81,290**

Production

TIMEFRAME: 50 shooting days over 6 months

CATEGORY/LINE ITEM	Amount	Units	Rate	Sub-Total	In-Kind	Deferred	Cash Needed
1.00 PERSONNEL							
1.10 Producer/director (Joiner)	6	months	5,000	30,000		10,000	20,000
1.11 Producer/director (Martin)	6	months	5,000	30,000		10,000	20,000
1.12 Co-producer/line producer	6	months	4,500	27,000		9,000	18,000
1.13 Executive producer(s)	1	allow	10,000	10,000		5,000	5,000
1.30 Production mgr	25	weeks	1,800	45,000		22,500	22,500
1.31 Office assistant/intern	120	hours	15	1,800			1,800
1.40 Cinematographer	65	days	650	42,250		14,083	28,167
1.41 Sound recordist	65	days	400	26,000		8,667	17,333
1.42 Production assistant/grip	50	days	275	13,750			13,750
1.52 Archival researcher	12	days	350	4,200			4,200
1.61 Assistant editor/digitizer	32	days	250	8,000			8,000
Total Personnel				238,000		79,250	158,750
2.00 EQUIPMENT RENTAL							
2.10 Sony HD900-R	65	days	1,200	78,000			78,000
2.20 ARRI light kit	20	weeks	300	6,000			6,000
2.30 Audio gear (mixer, mikes, etc.)	65	days	150	9,750			9,750
2.50 Specialty rentals	1	allow	2,500	2,500			2,500
2.61 Storage media	1	allow	7,500	7,500			7,500
2.62 Studio	12	days	800	9,600			9,600
Total Equipment				113,350			113,350
3.00 TRAVEL							
3.10 Airfare	64	RT tickets	600	38,400	5,760		32,640
3.11 Excess baggage fees	16	trips	250	4,000			4,000
3.20 Per diem	224	person-days	45	10,080			10,080
3.30 Accommodation	168	nights	300	50,400			50,400
3.40 Ground transport	16	trips	400	6,400	1,000		5,400
3.50 Catering/hospitality	50	days	125	6,250			6,250
Total Travel				115,530	6,760		108,770
4.00 MATERIALS & SERVICES							
4.50 Fiscal sponsorship	1	allow	17,500	17,500			17,500
4.60 Accounting	1	allow	1,000	1,000			1,000
4.70 Legal	1	allow	1,500	1,500			1,500
4.80 Promotion	1	allow	2,500	2,500			2,500
Total Materials & Services				22,500			22,500

CATEGORY/LINE ITEM	Amount	Units	Rate	Sub-Total	In-Kind	Deferred	Cash Needed
5.00 ADMINISTRATIVE							
5.10 Office rental [incl. admin computers]	6	months	800	4,800	-	2,400	2,400
5.20 Internet/telecom	6	months	80	480	-	240	240
5.30 Photocopying/printing	1	allow	2,000	2,000	-	-	2,000
5.40 Postage/shipping	1	allow	1,000	1,000	-	-	1,000
5.50 Misc office expenses	1	allow	500	500	-	-	500
Total Administrative				8,780	-	2,640	6,140
6.00 INSURANCE							
6.10 Producer's pkg & gnl liability	1	allow	20,000	20,000	-	-	20,000
Total Insurance				20,000	-	-	20,000
PRODUCTION SUB-TOTAL				498,160	6,760	81,890	429,510
CONTINGENCY [estimated @ 10% of cash costs]							42,951
TOTAL PRODUCTION						$	472,461

Post-Production

TIMEFRAME: 8 months (some overlap with production)

CATEGORY/LINE ITEM	Amount	Units	Rate	Sub-Total	In-Kind	Deferred	Cash Needed
1.00 PERSONNEL							
1.10 Producer/director (Joiner)	8	months	5,000	40,000		13,333	26,667
1.11 Producer/director (Martin)	8	months	5,000	40,000		13,333	26,667
1.12 Coproducer/line producer	8	months	4,500	36,000		12,000	24,000
1.13 Executive producer(s)	1	allow	15,000	15,000		5,000	10,000
1.14 Writer(s)	3	weeks	2,500	7,500		2,500	5,000
1.31 Office assistant/intern	160	hours	15	2,400		-	2,400
1.33 Post supervisor	80	days	375	30,000		10,000	20,000
1.32 Transcription	600	hours	30	18,000		-	18,000
1.52 Archival researcher	25	days	350	8,750		-	8,750
1.60 Editor	30	weeks	3,000	90,000		30,000	60,000
1.61 Assistant editor/digitizer	4	weeks	1,000	4,000		-	4,000
1.62 Effects/photo animation	14	weeks	2,000	28,000		9,333	18,667
1.63 Sound mixer/designer	6	weeks	2,000	12,000		4,000	8,000
1.80 Narrator	10	hours	175	1,750		-	1,750
1.90 Consultants	80	hours	75	6,000		2,000	4,000
Total Personnel				339,400	-	101,500	237,900
2.00 EQUIPMENT RENTAL							
2.60 Editing system (Final Cut Pro)	26	weeks	250	6,500		-	8,500
2.61 Storage media	1	allow	2,000	2,000		-	2,000
2.62 Sound recording studio	3	days	500	1,500		-	1,500
Total Equipment				10,000	-	-	10,000
4.00 MATERIALS & SERVICES							
4.10 Online	3	weeks	10,000	30,000		-	30,000
4.11 HD upconversion/tape printing	1	allow	1,000	1,000		-	1,000
4.12 HD to film transfer	1	allow	35,000	35,000		-	35,000
4.20 Graphics/titles	1	allow	7,500	7,500		-	7,500
4.21 Captioning	1	allow	5,000	5,000		-	5,000
4.30 Archival clearance	20	minutes	1,500	30,000		-	30,000
4.40 Music composition/recording	1	allow	10,000	10,000		-	10,000
4.41 Music clearance	1	allow	10,000	10,000		-	10,000
4.50 Fiscal sponsorship	1	allow	1,400	1,400		-	1,400
4.60 Accounting	1	allow	2,500	2,500		-	2,500
4.70 Legal	1	allow	2,000	2,000		-	2,000
4.80 Promotion	1	allow	5,000	5,000		-	5,000
Total Materials & Services				139,400	-	-	139,400

CATEGORY/LINE ITEM	Amount	Units	Rate	Sub-Total	In-Kind	Deferred	Cash Needed
5.00 ADMINISTRATIVE							
5.10 Office rental (incl. admin computers)	6	months	800	4,800	-	-	4,800
5.20 Internet/telecom	6	months	80	480	-	-	480
5.30 Photocopying/printing	1	allow	500	500	-	-	500
5.40 Postage/shipping	1	allow	500	500	-	-	500
5.50 Misc office expenses	1	allow	500	500	-	-	500
Total Administrative				6,780	-	-	6,780
6.00 INSURANCE							
6.30 Errors & Omissions	1	allow	7,500	7,500	-	-	7,500
Total Insurance				7,500	-	-	7,500
POST-PRODUCTION SUB-TOTAL				495,580	-	101,500	401,580
CONTINGENCY [estimated @ 10% of cash costs]							40,158
TOTAL POST-PRODUCTION							$ 441,738

Distribution & Outreach

TIMEFRAME: 12 months (some overlap with post-production)

CATEGORY/LINE ITEM	Amount	Units	Rate	Sub-Total	In-Kind	Deferred	Cash Needed
1.00 PERSONNEL							
1.10 Producer/director (Joiner)	6	months	5,000	30,000	15,000	-	15,000
1.11 Producer/director (Martin)	6	months	5,000	30,000	15,000	-	15,000
1.12 Co-producer/line producer	6	months	4,500	27,000	13,500	-	13,500
1.31 Office assistant/intern	160	hours	18	2,880	-	-	2,880
1.61 Assistant editor	2	weeks	1,000	2,000	-	-	2,000
1.70 Web content, producer	18	weeks	2,000	36,000	-	-	36,000
1.71 Web design & programming	1	allow	25,000	25,000	-	-	25,000
1.72 Web manager/moderator	12	months	2,000	24,000	-	-	24,000
1.73 Web content, contributors	1	allow	10,000	20,000	15,000	-	5,000
Total Personnel				196,880	58,500	-	138,380
2.00 EQUIPMENT RENTAL							
2.60 Editing system (Final Cut Pro)	2	weeks	250	500	-	-	500
2.61 Storage media	1	allow	1,000	1,000	-	-	1,000
Total Equipment				1,500	-	-	1,500
3.00 TRAVEL							
3.10 Airfare	10	RT tickets	600	6,000	-	-	6,000
3.20 Per diem	30	person-days	50	1,500	-	-	1,500
3.30 Accommodation	15	nights	200	3,000	600	-	2,400
3.40 Ground transport	10	trips	100	1,000	400	-	600
Total Travel				11,500	1,000	-	10,500
4.00 MATERIALS & SERVICES							
4.50 Fiscal sponsorship	1	allow	1,400	1,400	-	-	1,400
4.60 Accounting	1	allow	1,000	1,000	-	-	1,000
4.70 Legal	1	allow	1,000	1,000	-	-	1,000
4.80 Promotion	1	allow	20,000	20,000	-	-	20,000
4.82 Dubs/screeners	1	allow	3,000	3,000	-	-	3,000
Total Materials & Services				26,400	-	-	26,400

CATEGORY/LINE ITEM	Amount	Units	Rate	Sub-Total	In-Kind	Deferred	Cash Needed
5.00 ADMINISTRATIVE							
5.10 Office rental (incl. admin computers)	10	months	800	8,000	-	-	8,000
5.20 Internet/telecom	10	months	80	800	-	-	800
5.30 Photocopying/printing	1	allow	2,000	2,000	-	-	2,000
5.40 Postage/shipping	1	allow	1,500	1,500	-	-	1,500
5.50 Misc office expenses	1	allow	500	500	-	-	500
Total Administrative				12,800	-	-	12,800
DISTRIBUTION & OUTREACH SUB-TOTAL				*249,080*	*59,500*	-	*189,580*
CONTINGENCY (estimated @ 10% of cash costs)							*18,958*
TOTAL DISTRIBUTION & OUTREACH							**$ 208,538**

BEHIND THE VELVET CURTAIN

Aquarius Media
2261 Market Street #502
San Francisco, CA 94114
(415) 255-2716
aquarius-media.com

SELECT BIBLIOGRAPHY

What follows is a short list of helpful fundraising resources. For a much more extensive list that is updated regularly, come to my Web site: *www.warshawski.com*

Publications

Cones, John W. *43 Ways to Finance Your Feature Film: A Comprehensive Analysis of Film Finance.* Southern Illinois University Press.

Davies, Adam P. and Nicol Wistreich. *The Film Finance Handbook: How to Fund Your Film: New Global Edition.* Netribution.

Dean, Carole Lee. *The Art of Film Funding: Alternative Financing Concepts.* Michael Wiese Productions.

Klein, Kim. *Fundraising for Social Change.* Chardon Press.

Laloggia, Nicole and Eden Wurmfeld. *IFP/West Independent Filmmaker's Manual.* Focal Press. Includes a CD Rom.

Lee, John J. *The Producer's Business Handbook.* Focal Press.

Levison, Louise. *Filmmakers and Financing: Business Plans for Independents.* Butterworth-Heinemann.

Litwak, Mark. *Dealmaking in the Film and Television Industry: From Negotiations to Final Contracts.* Silman-James Press.

Lukk, Tiiu. *Movie Marketing: Opening the Picture and Giving It Legs.* Silman-James Press.

Robinson, Andy. *Grassroots Grants: An Activist's Guide to Proposal Writing.* Jossey-Bass, 1996.

Simon, Deke and Michael Wiese. *Film and Video Budgets.* 4th updated edition. Michael Wiese Productions.

Squire, Jason E., ed. *The Movie Business Book.* Third edition. Fireside/Simon & Schuster.

Vachon, Christine and David Edelstein. *Shooting to Kill: How an Independent Producer Blasts Through the Barriers to Make Movies That Matter.* Avon Books.

Warshawski, Morrie. *The Fundraising Houseparty: How to Party with a Purpose and Raise Money for Your Cause — 2nd Edition.* Available from the author, *www.warshawski.com.*

Warwick, Mal. *Revolution in the Mailbox, Revised Edition.* Jossey-Bass Publishers.

————. *How to Write Successful Fundraising Letters, Second Edition.* Jossey-Bass Publishers.

————. *The Mercifully Brief, Real-World Guide to Raising $1,000 Gifts by Mail.* Emerson & Church Publishers.

Wiese, Michael. *The Independent Film and Videomaker's Guide.* Michael Wiese Productions.

Helpful Web Sites

Association of Fundraising Professionals
www.afpnet.org

Box Office Mojo
www.boxofficemojo.com

The Chronicle of Philanthropy
www.philanthropy.com

The Council on Foundations
www.cof.org

Doculink
www.doculink.org

The D-Word
www.d-word.com

European Documentary Network
www.edn.dk

Fiscal Sponsor Directory
www.fiscalsponsordirectory.org

The Foundation Center
www.fdncenter.org

Foundations On Line
www.foundations.org

The Fund for Women Artists
www.womenarts.org/

Grantsnet/ U.S. Department of Health and Human Services
www.hhs.gov/grantsnet

Media Rights.ORG
www.mediarights.org

Mal Warwick Associates
www.malwarwick.com

Morrie Warshawski's Fundraising Bibliography
www.warshawski.com

National Alliance for Media Arts and Culture
www.namac.org

National Assembly of State Arts Agencies
www.nasaa-arts.org

New York Foundation for the Arts/ Interactive
www.nyfa.org

The Workbook Project
http://workbookproject.com/

Why Fund Media
www.fundfilm.org/for_media/for_media_ov.htm

ABOUT THE AUTHOR

Photo by Marissa Carlisle

Morrie Warshawski is a consultant, facilitator, and writer who specializes in helping nonprofit organizations on issues of strategic planning. His work is characterized by a commitment to the core values of creativity, tolerance, thoughtfulness, and transparency. Warshawski received a BA and MA in English from the University of Southern California, and attended the Graduate Writers Workshop in Iowa. His work in the nonprofit sector includes serving as the Executive Director of three arts organizations (Bay Area Video Coalition, Northwest Media Project, Portland Dance Theater) and, since 1986, as a consultant to a wide variety of clients including the National Endowment for the Arts, National Assembly of State Arts Agencies, Habitat for Humanity, Maryland State Arts Council, President's Committee on the Arts and Humanities, and many others.

As a writer, Warshawski's works have appeared in many journals and newspapers (*Emmy Magazine, Grantmakers in the Arts Newsletter, Los Angeles Times, Modern Poetry Studies, Parenting, San Francisco Examiner*). In addition to *Shaking the Money Tree*, his books include *The Fundraising Houseparty, The Next Step*, and *A State Arts Agency Planning Toolkit*.

Warshawski does consultations with independent filmmakers (in person and by phone) on issues of career development and fundraising plans. A full description of his "Initial Consultation" requirements and costs (along with upcoming travel plans for workshops and seminars) can be found on his Web site:

www.warshawski.com

If you are a filmmaker who wants assistance with fundraising, please be aware that Warshawski **does not** do any direct fundraising or grantwriting.

THE ART OF FILM FUNDING
ALTERNATIVE FINANCING CONCEPTS

CAROLE LEE DEAN

Learn winning techniques to get a "yes" from a woman who writes checks to independent filmmakers. This book will show you the inside track to funds from corporations and individuals to produce your films.

Here is the ultimate reference guide for creating the perfect pitch, inspiring your winning application, finding and connecting with funding organizations, making a successful "ask," and landing the money to make your film.

"Carole Dean has years of experience both as a producer and a funder, and her new book is full of nuts-and-bolts information from both sides of the fence, told in a conversational and heart-felt manner. Of special interest to filmmakers will be the in-depth interviews with experts in the field and an extensive appendix chock full of references. A great new addition to the filmmaker's lexicon."
— Morrie Warshawski, Consultant and Author, *Shaking the Money Tree*

"In The Art of Film Funding, *Carole Dean has assembled insights and wisdom that will prove immensely useful to filmmakers in their search for funding."*
— Mark Litwak, Attorney and Author, *Contracts for the Film and Television Industry*

"Packed full of information, juxtaposed with kind words and wisdom from a woman who has spent her life nurturing filmmakers."
— Barbara Trent, Academy Award® Winner, *The Panama Deception*

"This book is the most intelligent, insightful and comprehensive guide to finding the money that I have ever read. Carole Dean is the independent filmmaker's best friend!"
— Christopher Ward, Award-Winning Independent Filmmaker

"My hat's off to Carole Dean for writing The Art of Film Funding. *Written with a spiritual perspective and trust for your intuition, she not only acknowledges these creative forces, but rightfully honors the business process as an art in itself! What a joyful journey into filmmaking."*
— Wendy De Rycke, Indie Producer

CAROLE LEE DEAN runs one of the largest independent film grants in the U.S., where she reads hundreds of applications a year. Carole created an industry with film short ends and was the world's largest tape recycling supplier in NYC, L.A., and Chicago. She is the entrepreneurial producer of over 100 programs.

$26.95 · 272 PAGES · ORDER NUMBER 72RLS · ISBN: 9781932907315

THE WRITER'S JOURNEY
3RD EDITION

MYTHIC STRUCTURE FOR WRITERS

CHRISTOPHER VOGLER

BEST SELLER
OVER 170,000 COPIES SOLD!

See why this book has become an international best seller and a true classic. *The Writer's Journey* explores the powerful relationship between mythology and storytelling in a clear, concise style that's made it required reading for movie executives, screenwriters, playwrights, scholars, and fans of pop culture all over the world.

Both fiction and nonfiction writers will discover a set of useful myth-inspired storytelling paradigms (i.e., "The Hero's Journey") and step-by-step guidelines to plot and character development. Based on the work of Joseph Campbell, *The Writer's Journey* is a must for all writers interested in further developing their craft.

The updated and revised third edition provides new insights and observations from Vogler's ongoing work on mythology's influence on stories, movies, and man himself.

"This book is like having the smartest person in the story meeting come home with you and whisper what to do in your ear as you write a screenplay. Insight for insight, step for step, Chris Vogler takes us through the process of connecting theme to story and making a script come alive."
> – Lynda Obst, Producer, *Sleepless in Seattle, How to Lose a Guy in 10 Days;*
> Author, *Hello, He Lied*

"This is a book about the stories we write, and perhaps more importantly, the stories we live. It is the most influential work I have yet encountered on the art, nature, and the very purpose of storytelling."
> – Bruce Joel Rubin, Screenwriter, *Stuart Little 2, Deep Impact,*
> *Ghost, Jacob's Ladder*

CHRISTOPHER VOGLER is a veteran story consultant for major Hollywood film companies and a respected teacher of filmmakers and writers around the globe. He has influenced the stories of movies from *The Lion King* to *Fight Club* to *The Thin Red Line* and most recently wrote the first installment of *Ravenskull*, a Japanese-style manga or graphic novel. He is the executive producer of the feature film *P.S. Your Cat is Dead* and writer of the animated feature *Jester Till*.

$26.95 · 300 PAGES · ORDER NUMBER 76RLS · ISBN: 193290736x

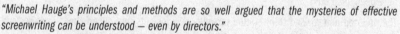

THE MYTH OF MWP

In a dark time, a light bringer came along, leading the curious and the frustrated to clarity and empowerment. It took the well-guarded secrets out of the hands of the few and made them available to all. It spread a spirit of openness and creative freedom, and built a storehouse of knowledge dedicated to the betterment of the arts.

The essence of the Michael Wiese Productions (MWP) is empowering people who have the burning desire to express themselves creatively. We help them realize their dreams by putting the tools in their hands. We demystify the sometimes secretive worlds of screenwriting, directing, acting, producing, film financing, and other media crafts.

By doing so, we hope to bring forth a realization of 'conscious media' which we define as being positively charged, emphasizing hope and affirming positive values like trust, cooperation, self-empowerment, freedom, and love. Grounded in the deep roots of myth, it aims to be healing both for those who make the art and those who encounter it. It hopes to be transformative for people, opening doors to new possibilities and pulling back veils to reveal hidden worlds.

MWP has built a storehouse of knowledge unequaled in the world, for no other publisher has so many titles on the media arts. Please visit www.mwp.com where you will find many free resources and a 25% discount on our books. Sign up and become part of the wider creative community!

Onward and upward,

Michael Wiese
Publisher/Filmmaker